DATA SCIENCE FROM SCRATCH WITH PYTHON
Step-by-Step Guide

Peter Morgan

AI SCIENCES

How to contact us

Please address comments and questions concerning this book to our customer service by email at:

contact@aisciences.net

Our goal is to provide high-quality books for your technical learning in computer science subjects.

Thank you so much for buying this book.

AI SCIENCES

Table of Contents

v

Edited by Davies Company
Ebook Converted and Cover by Pixels Studio
Publised by AI Sciences LLC

ISBN-13: 978-1726020688
ISBN-10: 1726020681

To my mom Janette

Author Biography

Peter Morgan is a lecturer at the Data Science Institute at Melbourne and a long-time Python user and developer. Peter worked also as a Machine Learning Scientist at Google for many years.

From AI Sciences Publisher

Chao Pan

John Anderson

Jonathan Adam

Michael Walker

WWW.AISCIENCES.NET

EBooks, free offers of eBooks and online learning courses.

Did you know that AI Sciences offers free eBooks versions of every book published? Please subscribe to our email list to be aware about our free eBook promotion. Get in touch with us at contact@aisciences.net for more details.

At www.aisciences.net , you can also read a collection of free books and received exclusive free eBooks.

Preface

"Data is a precious thing and will last longer than the systems themselves."

— *Tim Berners-Lees*

If you are looking for a complete guide to data science using Python from scratch, step by step, this book is for you.

Why the AI Sciences Books are different?

The AI Sciences Books explore every aspect of Artificial Intelligence and Data Science using computer Science programming language such as Python and R. Our books may be the best one for beginners; it's a step-by-step guide for any person who wants to start learning Artificial Intelligence and Data Science from scratch. It will help you in preparing a solid foundation and learn any other high-level courses will be easy to you.

Step-by-Step Guide and Visual Illustrations and Examples

The Book give complete instructions for manipulating, processing, cleaning, modeling and crunching datasets in Python. This is a hands-on guide with practical case studies of data analysis problems effectively. You will learn pandas, NumPy, IPython, and Jupiter in the Process.

Who Should Read This?

This book presents the foundational principles guiding the relatively new field of data science. It also utilises a practical learning approach where readers are encouraged to experiment with code snippets and arrive at conclusions that deepen the learning process. Data science has been termed the sexiest job of the 21st century by Harvard Business Review and as such it is clear that large swathes of people are trying to gain the skills needed to stand out in this exciting field that promises answers to a myriad of questions. The following groups of people would benefit maximally from from this book:

- The reader who has heard about the impact data science is set to make across industries but isn't quite sure what skills are required to get a footing in the field. This set of readers can expect to profit from the clear explanations of basic concepts and build intuitions that enable them transition on to more complex topics.

- The practitioner who has intermediate level skills in the related fields of statistics, mathematics, computer science and machine learning but wants to understand in what ways data science is a different discipline. This type of reader would understand the concepts presented in this book quickly as data science is an interdisciplinary field that sits at the intersection between many well established scientific fields. At the end of this book, the reader would have a toolbelt of skills to transition into a data science role.

- The practicing data scientist or experienced veteran would appreciate this book for providing a refresher on many common concepts and a whirlwind tour of what is currently obtainable in terms of best practices. The breadth of this book is such that this reader would have a reference manual of sorts for how to implement data science techniques using modern tools.

The book is structured into two main parts. The first part presents a theoretical overview of the underlying principles on which the entire data science stack is based. This includes sections about statistics, probability and machine learning. The second half of the book is mainly practical. It includes hands on tutorials which shows real world implementations of the techniques and algorithms discussed in part one. The reader is advised to work along when reading the second part of the book as practice enables concepts to take on real meaning.

Regardless of the level of expertise of the reader, be it a beginner or a seasoned professional, there are lots of distilled knowledge available in these pages which would give the reader a new perspective on what data science is all about.

Why this book?

This book is written to help you learn data analysis using Python programming. If you are an absolute beginner in this field, you'll find that this book explains complex concepts in an easy to understand manner without math or complicated theorical elements. If you are an experienced data scientist, this book gives you a good base from which to explore data analysis applications.

Topics are carefully selected to give you a broad exposure to data analysis application. While not overwhelming you with information overload.

The example and cases studies are carefully chosen to demonstrate each algorithm and model so that you can gain a deeper understand of data analysis. Inside the book and in the appendices at the end of the book we provide you a convenient references.

You can download the source code for the project at:

http://aisciences.net/book3

Your Free Gifts

As a way of saying thanks you for your purchase, AI Sciences Publishing Company offers you a free eBook in Machine Learning with Python written by the data scientist Alain Kaufmann.

It is a full book that contains useful machine learning techniques using python. It is a 100 page book with one bonus chapter focusing on Anaconda Setup & Python Crash Course. AI Sciences encourage you to print, save and share. <u>You can download it by going to the link below</u> or by clicking in the book cover above.

<u>http://aisciences.net/free-books/</u>

AI Sciences Publishing Company offers you a free eBook in Introduction to Python for Data Analysis written by Robert Danboard.

It is a full introduction book in Python for Data Analysis. It is a 100 pages book. AI Sciences encourage you to print, save and share. You can download it by going to the link below or by clicking in the book cover above.

http://aisciences.net/free-book-3/

If you want to help us produce more material like this, then please leave an honest review on amazon. It really does make a difference.

https://www.amazon.com/dp/B07F7QC635

What is Data Science?

Data science is multidisciplinary field that relies on scientific methods, statistics and algorithms to extract meaningful insights from data. At its core, data science is all about discovering useful patterns in data that can then be presented as information to tell a story or make informed decisions. It would be noticed that data science depends on techniques from a bunch of other fields such as computer science, mathematics, statistics and business analytics. It is common for data scientists to have skills across this range. Data science can be employed to derive insights from both small and large datasets and it is often a misconception that data science is only suited to so called big data.

Let us have a look at the venn diagram below that gives an overview of the intersection of data science with other fields. The venn diagram was popularized by data scientist Drew Conway as his definition of data science.

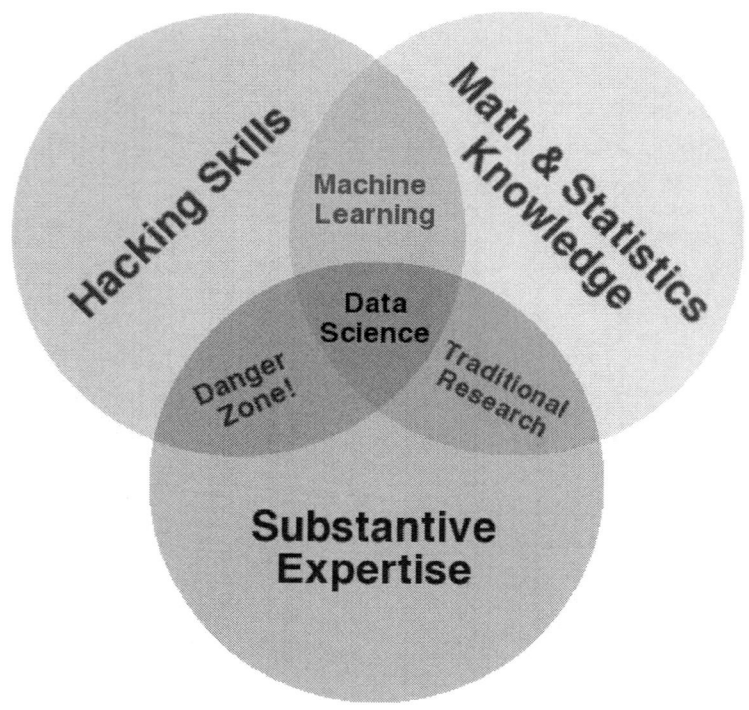

In the diagram, we can see that there are three main blobs or circles, each representing some distinct field. Hacking skills can be seen as the domain of computer science and information technology. The second field is mathematics and statistics which provide various rigorous theories as relates to equations and explanations. The last major field is substantive expertise. This can be seen as domain expertise or business knowledge. It includes the underlying business or domain logic peculiar to a specific kind of problem.

The intersection between hacking skills and mathematics/statistics is machine learning. Machine learning relies heavily on techniques in the fields of computer science and mathematics. It is a subfield of artificial intelligence.

The second intersection is traditional research. Traditional research typically utilizes techniques from mathematics and statistics combined with domain expertise to arrive at new conclusions. This intersection is responsible for many discoveries made in the past.

Danger skills can actually be seen as the realm of traditional software development where a person combines knowledge about a business problem and computer science skills such as coding to fabricate software which bring about additional value to a process.

Data science is at the inner intersection. It is a combination of all the aforementioned skills whereby techniques from these related fields are mashed in such a way that value can be created from data in the form of identifying patterns which drive predictive outcomes. Data science enables the realization of findings from data which propels businesses to make smarter decisions based on insights so unearthed, such as understanding customer behaviours, inferring customer decisions and spotting trends earlier in their cycle.

Data science has existed in many forms throughout recent history although it has only now been coalesced into a field of its own. In the past, different professionals worked with data in one capacity or the other. These jobs included business analysts, statisticians, data analysts, computer scientists etc. Even Though data scientists today still perform a number of roles similar to those previously described, data science goes a step further by trying to make discovered insights actionable in terms of predictive use cases. This clear goal of driving insights into production is one of the distinguishing characteristics of data science when compared to other analytical fields.

Data Science Applications

Data science is a very practical field with several real world applications ranging from consumer facing products to industrial products. We take a look at a few popular applications of data science in order to get a taste of its awesome power.

Fraud Detection

Many financial institutions deploy data science in their validation pipeline to automatically flag suspicious credit or debit card transactions. Data collected from consumers over several years of financial services being rendered is scrutinized to uncover patterns that may indicate financial impropriety. The model is constructed in a way that it learns to identify high risk features and automatically predicts that a fraud is likely to be perpetrated. Every new transaction is now run against a trained model which categorizes it as being normal or fraudulent. Transactions identified as fraudulent may be blocked by the system or referred to a human employee for further investigation. The features of such a fraud detection system are details of the transaction example the location of the transaction, amount, credit score of participants, credit card status etc. All of these provide information that is used by the model to correctly arrive at a suitable classification. An extension of this application could be in loan request approval, where a financial institution could decide to approve or turn down loan requests by customers based on patterns learnt from past loan applications. Data science is heavily used in finance because it automates the process of analyzing financial transactions, not only saving time and resources but it also identifies correlations that may not be immediately visible to a team of human experts.

Recommender Systems

Recommender systems also known as recsys are a way of providing product recommendation to users based on past preferences or other user information. They solve the problem of relevance as users are usually faced with decision paralysis when bombarded with a choice spectrum. Data science uses explicit and implicit user feedback to build a personalized profile of each user so that a user is likely to see content that they are most likely to be interested in. A prominent area where recommender systems are heavily used is in the e-commerce sector. Products are automatically recommended to users based on what has been purchased. In some cases, products purchased by users with a similar taste as the current user, are shown higher up in a listing as it is has been proven that clusters of customers with similar preferences are likely to enjoy the same offerings.

Recommender systems are used by companies like Netflix and Amazon to finetune content shown to end users, thereby driving adoption and sales respectively.

Image Recognition

Data science and machine learning currently power image recognition systems where the learning problem is to correctly identify objects in an image. This has loads of applications and is used by Facebook to automatically tag friends in uploaded images. Face recognition is also used by security systems to identify and grant access to authorized persons in a restricted area. Another application of image recognition techniques is in image search as experienced on Google Photos. We can search for images with particular kinds of events in them such as birthdays for example.

Digital Advertising

A highly profitable application of data science which completely disrupted an entire industry is digital advertising. Digital advertisements have shaken up the marketing landscape by providing targeted personalized ads which have a far greater conversion rate when compared to traditional advertising. This high return on investment is as a result of data science algorithms understanding a user and presenting advertisements that they are likely to find informative and useful. Instead of the one size fits all approach of traditional advertisements, digital adverts backed by a data science process displays adverts that are relevant to an individual user.

The above applications are not an exhaustive list of data science applications as there are many other areas not covered like delivery logistics, speech recognition, internet search, customer churn etc. It should now be clear that the applications of data science are numerous and there are other domains where data science has not yet been applied to.

Why Use Python for Data Science

There are many tools and programming languages that facilitate the practice of data science such as R, Python, SAS, SQL, Apache Hadoop etc. The two most popular languages in the data science world are R and Python. R is mainly favored by statisticians while Python is generally used by computer scientists and software engineers. The main benefit of using Python is that it is a general purpose programming language that is expressive and supports fast prototyping. The nature of Python as a general programming language means that an entire data science stack can be built in a single language from prototyping and experimentation to building web applications and deployment. The other major benefit of using Python is that it has a vibrant scientific community behind it and has several mature scientific computation libraries.

In recent years, Python has slowly overtaken R as the major language used in data science because of the reasons highlighted above. Also, recent machine learning techniques such as deep learning have more matured frameworks in Python as compared to R. This has helped tilt the balance in favour of Python. As we would see in the second half of this book which deals with practical examples, the syntax of Python is really easy to pick up and good functionality can be implemented in few lines of code.

Types of Data

There are two distinct types of data namely categorical and numerical. Categorical data are data types that can be separated into groups or categories. Under categorical data, we have two subtypes - nominal and ordinal. Nominal data is where there is no innate ordering of categories example male and female whereas ordinal data is categorical data that has a concept of ordering example small, medium, large. Numerical data on the other hand involves data whose values can be measured. There are also two subtypes for numerical data namely discrete and continuous. Discrete data can be counted and its values are discrete or separate example number of rooms in a house. Continuous data are those numerical data which can take on any value in a finite or infinite range example height of a person. The main difference between discrete and continuous data is that discrete data can only take on integer values (whole numbers) whereas continuous data could be any value.

Data may be accessed in different forms such as structured, unstructured, natural language, audio, video, images etc. Structured data usually has a fixed form or description such as tables contained in a database while unstructured data as the name implies doesn't have an inherent structure and its content is context specific. Unstructured data is usually high dimensional and more difficult to process than structured data.

Big Data

There are three main features that distinguish big data from other types of data. They are volume, variety and velocity. Collectively they are referred to as the three Vs. Volume signifies that the amounts of data being dealt with is very large, variety indicates that there are different types of data present while velocity denotes the speed at which this data is generated and how quickly it is required to be analyzed. In some cases a fourth V, veracity is introduced. This gives an inkling of how accurate the data is. Together, these properties of big data make it nearly impossible for it to be handled by traditional data management tools.

Big data tools can be classified into storage and analysis tools. Some popular big data tools are Apache Hadoop, Hive, Spark, NoSQL etc. Data science as a discipline is increasingly tackling many of the challenges occasioned by the dawn of big data such as data capture, storage, search, visualization etc.

Statistics

Data in Statistics

Many data science modelling techniques have their roots in statistics. Statistics is a field of mathematics that deals with presenting information garnered from data in a form that is easy to understand. It involves collection, analysis, organization and presentation of data. Simply put statistics enable us draw a summary of our raw data. This presentation of gleaned information is usually done in graphs, charts, tables etc. Data can be seen as raw facts from which we can draw conclusions while statistics is the process through which we employ numerical and mathematical techniques to actually derive knowledge from data. Even Though both are related, there is a clear distinction between them. Data in an unprocessed form is not informative but barely contains the building blocks through which we can use statistics to transform it into information that is relevant. Information is data that has been processed to give meaning. This may take the mould of classification or correlations.

There are two main branches of statistics - descriptive and inferential. Descriptive statistics is concerned with summarizing a sample population in terms of indices such as mean, mode, standard deviation whereas inferential statistics is interested in arriving at conclusions from the data by studying the underlying probability distribution that makes the data unique.

Descriptive and Inferential Statistics

Descriptive statistics is the branch of statistics that is interested in describing the nature of data as a direct effect of the population under study. The population under study are made of samples and those samples are usually complete and can be used to study that population effectively. The role of descriptive statistics is to summarize the characteristics of the population. There are two broad techniques employed - measures of central tendencies and measures of spread. Measures of central tendencies like mean, mode and median gives the most common occurrences in the data whereas measures of spread like variance, range, quartiles, standard deviation etc describe how far samples are from the central position. Descriptive statistics techniques are mainly used to organize, analyze and present data in a meaningful way.

However, in most cases, we do not have access to the entire data in a population. We can merely collect a subset of data that is representative of the wider population. In such cases, we would like to use our sample data to model aspects of the wider population. This is where inferential statistics come in. Inferential statistics is the branch of statistics that seeks to arrive at conclusions about a population through the analysis of sample data that is drawn from that population. It discovers trends within a sample and then tries to generalize those trends to the wider population. Inferential statistics is made up of two parts, estimation of parameters and testing out hypothesis. The results of inferential statistics are usually presented as probabilities that show the confidence of particular parameters or events being true. In a nutshell, inferential statistics is concerned with making predictions about a population through the study of a sample from that population.

Measures of Central Tendencies

In descriptive statistics, we often want to measure the properties that describe the distribution (population), this is done in terms of two properties, the central tendency and dispersion. The population central tendency encompasses the typical (common) value of the distribution. From the normal distribution or bell curve, the common type of value is usually at the center hence the name central tendency.

Let at look at the diagram below which contains some measures of central tendencies to hone our intuitions further.

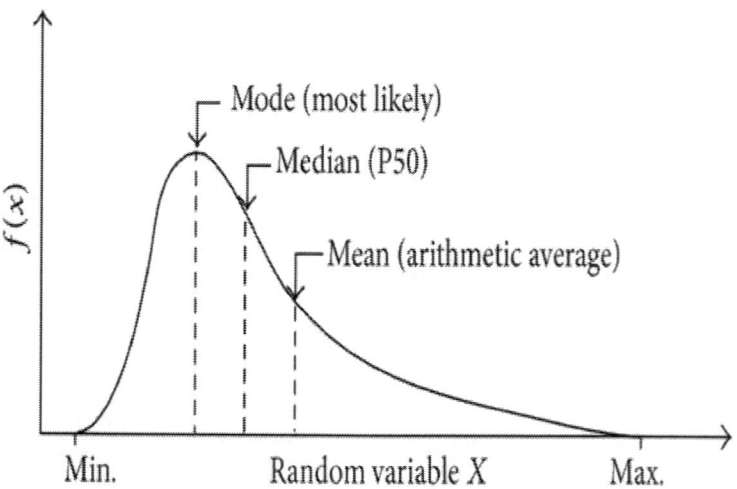

The plot contains data from an independent variable X in some distribution. The role of measures of central tendencies is to describe common or typical values of the sample population. We can see that the highest point in the 2-dimensional plot of the independent variable against the dependent variable is the mode. The mode indicates the most likely value in the distribution, in other words, it is the most popular or frequently occuring value in the dataset. The median is the midway point between all values after they have been arranged in ascending or descending order. The midway point usually occurs at the 50% mark. The mean or arithmetic average is the ratio of the sum of all values to the number of values in the population. It is given by the formula below:

$$A = \frac{1}{n} \sum_{i=1}^{n} a_i = \frac{a_1 + a_2 + \cdots + a_n}{n}$$

Where A = arithmetic mean

n = number of observations and

a = individual observation

Together, the arithmetic mean, mode and median give a good description of a dataset and are frequently used in descriptive statistics.

Let us now look at how we can compute central tendencies on a toy dataset.

First we import Numpy and Scipy.

```
import numpy as np
from scipy import stats
```

Next we create a dataset by passing a list into Numpy array function.

```
dataset = np.array([3, 1, 4, 1, 1])
```

We can easily calculate the mean by calling the mean function from Numpy and passing in the dataset.

```
mean = np.mean(dataset)
print(mean)
```

```
Mean: 2.0
```

To calculate the median, we call the median function from Numpy and pass in the dataset.

```
median = np.median(dataset)
print('Median: {:.1f}'.format(median))
```

```
Median: 1.0
```

Finally, to compute the mode, we use the mode function from Scipy stats module.

```
mode= stats.mode(dataset)
print(mode)
print('Mode: {}'.format(mode[0][0]))
print('{} appeared {} times in the dataset'.format(mode[0][0],
mode[1][0]))
```

```
ModeResult(mode=array([1]), count=array([3]))
Mode: 1.0
1.0 appeared 3 times in the dataset
```

The mode is 1 since it is the most common number in our toy dataset.

Dispersion, Covariance and Correlation

The dispersion of a distribution refers to how widely spread sample data points are in that population. It explains the amount of variability present in a distribution, that is how widely do data points vary across across a central location.

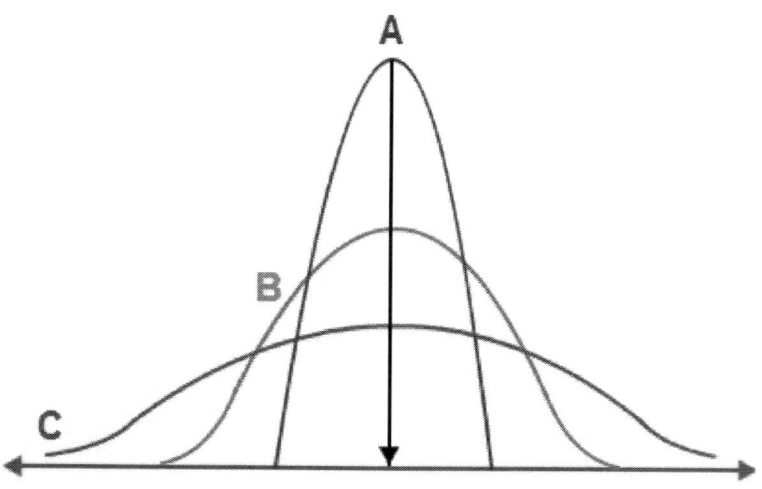

In the image above, distribution A has low dispersion. This is because most of its values are centered in the middle. It should be noted that the centrality of data points has an inverse relationship with dispersion. In distribution B, there is greater dispersion as values appear to be located across a broader range. The shorter height of the curve when compared to A shows that its mean is lower as values are not compact within a central range. Distribution C shows the most variation. The values are spread across a greater range than A or B and its height is very low indicating small values for measures of central tendency such as the mean. Some ways in which statistical dispersion is measured includes variance, standard deviation and interquartile range.

The formula for standard deviation is given below:

$$SD = \sqrt{\frac{\sum |x - \mu|^2}{N}}$$

It should be noted that variance is the square of standard deviation.

The variance as we have seen defines how much values of a variable are away from its mean. That is how greatly does it vary across the distribution. Covariance extends the concept of variance from one variable to two variables. Covariance measures how well two random variables vary in line with each other.

The formula for covariance is given by:

$$\text{cov}(X,Y) = \frac{\sum_{i=1}^{n}(X_i - \bar{X})(Y_i - \bar{Y})}{n-1}$$

The covariance of X and Y tells us how much a change in X results in a corresponding change in Y. The covariance paints a picture about the relationship between random variables and how they interact with each other. Despite its ability to indicate relationship between random variables, the covariance does not tell us by what degree variables are correlated. This is because random variables may be in different units and there is no way we would be able to interpret it deeply without knowing the extent of the relationship. Covariance merely tells us whether variables are positively or negatively correlated, there is no actual meaning attached to the size of the computation result (number indicating covariance). To solve this problem we use another measure known as the correlation.

The correlation is defined as the covariance normalized (divided) by the square root of the product of the variance of each random variable.

The mathematical formula for the definition of correlation is shown below:

$$r_{xy} = \frac{\sum\limits_{i=1}^{n}(x_i - \bar{x})(y_i - \bar{y})}{\sqrt{\sum\limits_{i=1}^{n}(x_i - \bar{x})^2 \sum\limits_{i=1}^{n}(y_i - \bar{y})^2}}$$

Correlation is a dimensionless quantity as the units in the numerator and denominator cancel out. The values for correlation lies in the range -1 to 1. With 1 indicating that there is positive correlation between variables and -1 indicating negative correlation. As a result of the normalizing effect of the denominator when calculating correlation, it gives us a good sense of the degree to which variables are related.

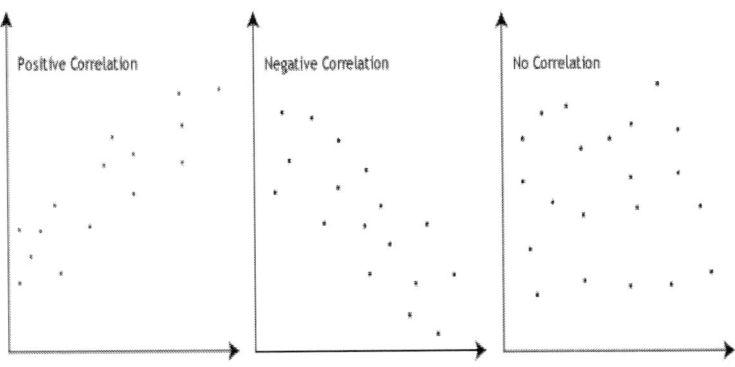

In the figure above, the first plot shows positive correlation between two variables in a 2-dimensional plane. What it means is that as the independent variable on the horizontal axis increases, the dependent variable on the vertical axis also increases. If we trace the set of points, we can see that the direction of movement is upwards. The second plot depicts negative correlation. As the independent variable increases on the x-axis, the dependent variable decreases down the y-axis. Similarly, if we trace the direction of points, we would notice that it tends downwards towards the negative side of the plot. This is how we know that the variables are negatively

31

correlated. Finally, in the last case, we see a plot that has no identifiable patterns, the distribution of both variables are not related to each other. An increase or decrease in one variable does not cause a corresponding shift in the other. We therefore conclude that the third plot shows no correlation between variables.

Let us now see how covariance and correlation can be implemented in Python using Numpy and Scipy.

We would create dummy data using Numpy random function which creates data from a uniform distribution.

```
import numpy as np
x = np.random.normal(size=2)
y = np.random.normal(size=2)
```

We stack x and y vertically to produce z using the line of code below.

```
z = np.vstack((x, y))
```

The data in now in the correct form and we can pass it to Numpy covariance function.

```
c = np.cov(z.T)
print(c)
```

```
[[ 0.08652802 -0.02009744]
 [-0.02009744  0.00466794]]
```

The result may be slightly different in your case because we are generating data points randomly.

To calculate correlation, let us import **pearsonr** from Scipy stats module and define a very simple dataset. The function imported is the Pearson correlation coefficient.

```
from scipy.stats.stats import pearsonr
a = [1, 4, 6]
b = [1, 2, 3]

corr = pearsonr(a, b)
print(corr)
```

```
(0.99339926779878274, 0.073186395040328034)
```

We can see that a and b are positively correlated as expressed by the coefficient 0.99, which is very close to 1.

Probability

Dependence and Independence

Probability is a measure of how likely we feel an event would occur. Probability is therefore a measure of likelihood. It is usually a value between 0 and 1 with 0 indicating impossibility, that is the event would never occur and 1 means certainty, the event is sure to occur.

In probability, two events are said to be dependent if the occurrence of the first event directly affects the probability of the second event occurring. This means that dependent events are reliant on each other. For the second event to happen the first must have occurred. Dependent events usually have an order to their occurence. In the same vein, random variables are said to be dependent if the actualization of one directly influences the probability distribution of the other. An example of dependent events are writing a book and getting published. To get published, you must first write a book. The probability of getting published directly depends on writing a book. The order is important as it cannot be changed. Writing a book must occur first before any publication.

Independent events are those events whose probability of occurrence are not dependent on each other. The fact that a first event has occurred does not in any way mean that a second event would occur or not. Both events are not linked as they are independent. To determine whether two events are independent, we first ask ourselves if both events can happen in any order. If the answer is yes, we ask ourselves a second question, does one event affect the outcome of the other. If the answer is no, then we have been able to prove that both events are completely independent of each other. An example of independent events are buying a new phone and eating your favorite meal. Those events are not dependent on each other. It is possible to imagine them occurring in any order. The fact that you just bought a new phone does not in any way affect the probability of you eating your favorite meal.

For two independent events lets say A and B. The probability of event A occurring given that event B has occurred is equal to the probability of A.

$$P(A \mid B) = P(A)$$

What this means is that whether or not event B has occurred, it does not affect the probability of A occurring because the probability of A is only dependent on itself, that is event A does not depend on external events. Similarly, the probability of event B given event A is equal to the probability of event B.

$$p(B \mid A) = P(B)$$

The probability of two independent events occurring is equal to the product of their individual probabilities.

$$P(A \cap B) = P(A) \cdot P(B)$$

Conditional Probability

Conditional probability can be defined as the measure of the probability of an event, say A occurring, given the knowledge that another event, say B, has occurred. Conditional probability deals with the probability of occurrence of an event in relation to other events. To define this formally, the probability of A given B is equal to the probability of the intersection of A and B (that is both events occur) divided by the probability of B.

$$P(A \mid B) = P(A \cap B)/P(B)$$

The term $P(A \mid B)$ is known as the conditional probability (probability of A given B), the numerator of the right hand side of the equation is the joint probability also called the probability of A and B. It should be noted that for independent events, the conditional probability of an event is equal to the probability of that same event. An understanding of conditional probability is vital as it is one of the fundamental concepts in probability theory and is used in the formulation of more complex concepts as we would see later.

Random Variables

Random variables as the name implies are those types of variables whose values are given by random processes. What this means is random variables maps the outcome of a random process to numbers that can be used in probability theory. An example of a random process is throwing a dice. The outcome is clearly random and cannot be predetermined. However, we can assign numbers to those random outcomes, the numbers so assigned would be quantities of a random variable. Random variables are also called random quantities or stochastic variables and are usually written in capital (uppercase) letters. Random variables are also measurable and contain numbers like regular variables in algebra but the key difference is that they are produced by a random process.

The definition of random variables also make it easier to use a compact notation when talking about random events. Example the probability of getting a number greater than 3 after rolling a dice once would be written as:

P(getting a number greater than 3 after rolling a dice once)

But if we define the random process using random variables, the notation can be simplified greatly:

X = getting a number greater than 3 after rolling a dice once

$P(X > 3)$

We can see that it becomes easier for us to calculate different outcomes without writing a lot of text. There are two types of random variables - discrete random variables and continuous random variables.

Discrete and Continuous Distributions

Discrete random variables are those random variables that can take on only a specific set of limited values which are all distinct. They are usually countable as they have a finite number of possible values. An example of discrete random variables are the outcomes from a dice. There is only a small set of values that a dice can produce, this makes it countable.

A discrete probability distribution is one that describes the probability associated with discrete random variables. That is it gives the probability of occurrence of discrete outcomes. The probability distribution of a discrete random variable is sometimes called the probability function or the probability mass function.

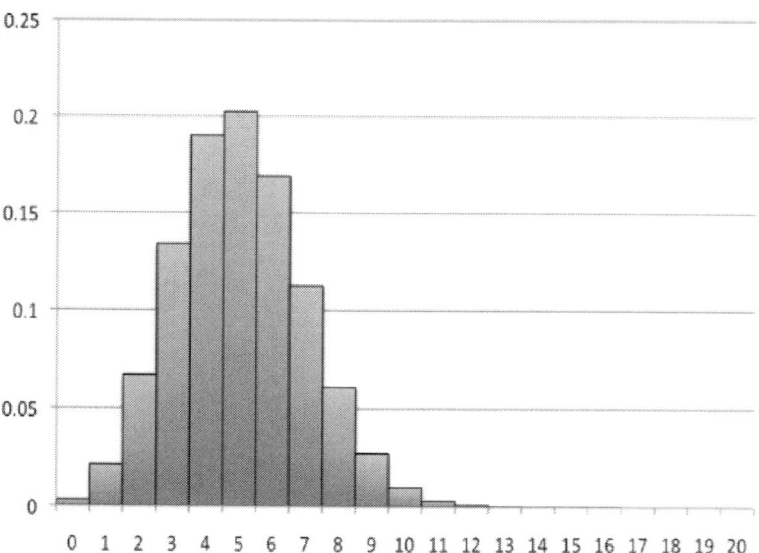

It would be observed from the above plot of a discrete probability distribution, that the probability of occurrence of a particular value of a random value is non-zero since the range of possibilities is finite. The type of plot above is known as a probability histogram. Examples of discrete probability distributions are binomial, poisson, hypergeometric etc.

Continuous random variables on the other hand can take on any possible value within an interval, that is it can take on an infinite number of values within a range. Continuous random variables are usually acquired through measurement such as the height of a person, weight or the salary of individuals in a company. In all these cases, the value can fall anywhere within a specified range.

A continuous probability distribution is associated with probabilities from continuous random variables. It describes the probability of possible values of a random variable. Continuous random variables are usually defined by an area under a curve and its distribution is non-zero for a range of values.

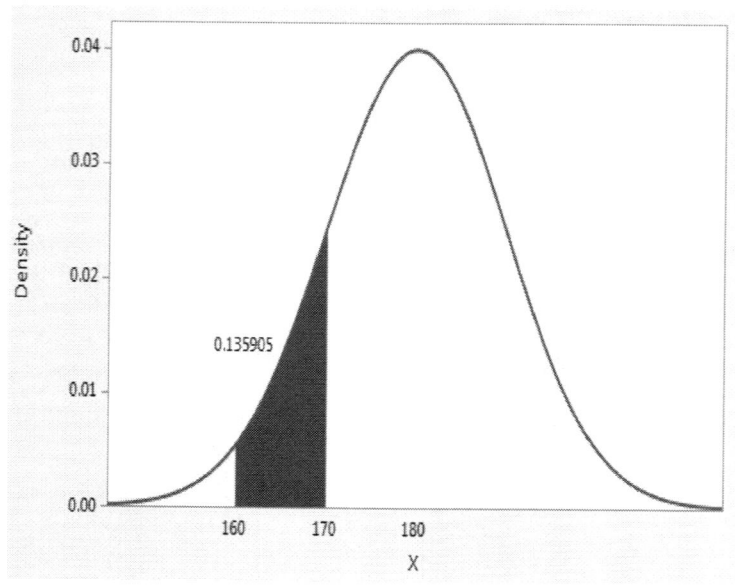

The probability distribution of random continuous variables are shown by a density curve similar to the one above. The probability of an exact value from the interval range of a continuous random variable is always zero. This is because by definition there are infinite values within the defined interval. The probability of a range can however be calculated by the area under the density curve.

Bayes' Theorem and Naive Bayes Algorithm

Bayes' theorem helps us calculate the conditional probability of related events. Bayes' theorem provides a way for us to update our belief system given the availability of new information or evidence. Using Bayes' theorem we can calculate the probability of an event A, given event B occurred, as the product of probability of B given A and the probability of A all divided by the probability of B.

$$P(A|B) = P(B|A)P(A)/P(B)$$

Where $p(A|B)$ is the conditional probability known as the posterior, that would represent our updated belief about the event occuring. $P(B|A)$ is the likelihood, how likely is B a result of event A. $P(A)$ is the prior, that is our understanding of the situation before we observed any data and $P(B)$ is known as the evidence.

Bayes' theorem is a powerful formulation because it allows us to get the conditional probabilities of events and update that probability (how likely is the event to occur) once we have new information or data. We first start with prior knowledge which in a way is a biased form of what is currently known. At each iteration, we can then update the posterior estimate using components of Bayes equation such as the likelihood, prior and evidence. Bayes' theorem is central to Bayesian statistics and has a wide range of applications.

Let us take a simple example that beautifully illustrates Bayes theorem. Say we draw a single card from a deck of playing cards, what is the probability that the card so drawn is a king, given evidence (additional information) whether it is a face card.

First let us define define Bayes theorem in line with the question.

P(King|Face) = P(Face|King)P(King)/P(Face)

Where;

P(King|Face) = probability the card is a king given it is a face card

P(Face|King) = probability the card is a face card given it is a king

P(King) = probability the card is a king

P(Face) = probability the card is a face card

Next we compute these probabilities and plug them into Bayes theorem.

The probability a drawn card is a king is 4/52, which is 1/13 because there are 4 kings and the total number of cards is 52.

Let's assume evidence is provided in the form of someone looking at the card. The person in this case confirms that the card is a face card. P(Face | King) becomes 1 because all kings are face cards (contains a face).

The last component is P(Face), there are 3 face types - Jack, Queen, King each of which has 4 cards, so P(Face) is 12/52 which reduces to 3/13.

We now have all the components and can now calculate the P(King | Face).

P(King | Face) = P(Face | King)P(King)/P(Face)

P(King | Face) = (1/13)(1)/(3/13) = 1/3

What P(King | Face) indicates is a way we can update our beliefs based on new evidence. As a result of new evidence that the card drawn is a face card, the probability that the card is a king given a face card jumps to ⅓ as compared with 1/13, which is the prior probability (when we had not observed evidence) that it was a king (P(King)). This example shows us that Bayes theorem gives us a way of calculating the posterior probability when we know the prior probability, the likelihood and evidence.

Naive Bayes algorithm is an application of Bayes' theorem as a classification algorithm with the explicit assumption that all features or predictors are independent. The word "naive" in its name is because of the independence assumption since we know that this is not always true and features tend to be related.

Naive Bayes algorithm relies on Bayes theorem which is stated mathematically as follows.

$$P(y \mid x_1, \ldots, x_n) = \frac{P(y)P(x_1, \ldots x_n \mid y)}{P(x_1, \ldots, x_n)}$$

With the independence assumption that all input features are unrelated, the numerator can be expressed as:

$$P(x_i \mid y, x_1, \ldots, x_{i-1}, x_{i+1}, \ldots, x_n) = P(x_i \mid y)$$

Using the independence representation, Bayes theorem can be simplified to a product of probabilities.

$$P(y \mid x_1, \ldots, x_n) = \frac{P(y) \prod_{i=1}^{n} P(x_i \mid y)}{P(x_1, \ldots, x_n)}$$

However, in our model, the input data remains constant, therefore the denominator has no effect on the model. We can choose to ignore it. Another way of thinking about it is that

44

there is no y term in the denominator, so it does not help us in any way to predict output classes. The formula then becomes a direct variation as shown below:

$$P(y \mid x_1, \ldots, x_n) \propto P(y) \prod_{i=1}^{n} P(x_i \mid y)$$

The final step is to cast it as an optimization operation where we need to maximize the probability of the correct class given the correct class and each input feature independently. The final formula for Naive Bayes algorithm becomes:

$$\hat{y} = \arg \max_{y} P(y) \prod_{i=1}^{n} P(x_i \mid y)$$

Despite its simplicity Naive Bayes algorithm is a very powerful classifier and is particularly useful as a multi-classification model. Naive Bayes is also very fast to run and performs very well when its independence assumption holds true compared to other algorithms. A popular use case of the Naive Bayes classifier is in email spam detection where the words of an email are regarded as independent features and the algorithm learns to categorize email into spam or not spam categories based on the content.

The Data Science Process

Asking the Right Question

The data science process starts with a simple premise - that there is a problem we want solved or insights we want to discover. This leads us to the very first step of any data science project. We need to understand what we are trying to achieve at a very deep level before we embark on the journey. This is encapsulated in asking the right question. What is the goal of this research endeavour, how does it benefit the business, in what ways would this provide better customer experience. Other questions include asking ourselves if there is a shortcoming that has been observed which we would like to find out more about.

Getting this stage right is the most important aspect of a data science project as all other steps flow from it. We do not want to have an ill defined problem, waste money and resources to prototype a supposed solution, only to discover that our solution does not solve the problem at hand simply because we did not understand what was required in the first place. It is therefore desirable that we explore as many hypotheses as possible and pit them against each other until we can narrow down the problem to a single question or research goal.

Some common questions in a data science project could be - who are our most valuable customers, what impact would changing our product have on customer satisfaction, can our data on customers help us predict their actions etc. If we look closely at these questions, we would notice a common trend. They all heavily involve knowledge about the business, that is they are all specific about our business domain. To formulate appropriate questions which would serve as the springboard for our data science projects, data scientists need not act in isolation because assumption at this stage is dangerous. The proper thing would be to involve those with a profound understanding of the business in the discussions by having a round table session where managers, marketers, customer service personnel etc elaborate on challenges that they may be facing. It is now the job of the data scientist to identify the underlying need and formulate that into a question that can be answered by data. If this is done correctly, everyone on the team knows what is expected or desired even before the project begins and this enables everyone to be on the same page and moderate their expectations.

It is also at this stage that a metric of success is set or put another way, how would we measure the success of the project. What would be an acceptable threshold and what is not. The measurement metric chosen is usually a direct reflection of how the data science question is framed. For example, accuracy could be selected as how the team would evaluate the final performance of the project. It is also important for everyone on board to understand that data science is not a silver bullet and there may be unforeseen circumstances that arise along the way.

Below is a schematic diagram of how the data science process looks. In the following sections we would explain each block in detail and show how they fit into a grand scheme.

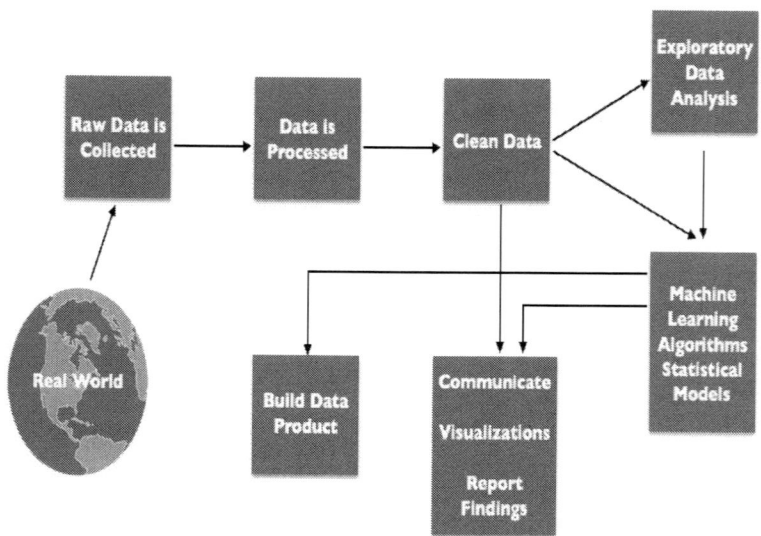

Data Acquisition

Immediately after we settle on a research goal, the next step is to acquire appropriate data through which we can begin to derive insights. The kind of data that is acquired is tailored towards the kind of problem we want to solve. By getting that particular type of data, we are making an assumption that the solution space provided by the data contains answers to our questions. We need to identify appropriate datasets if they already exist or most likely create one ourselves. The data acquisition step may include sourcing for data within the organization or leveraging external sources of data.

48

Data may come from relational databases, spreadsheets, inventories, external APIs etc. During this stage, it is reasonable to check that the data is in the correct format for our purposes. In-depth checks may not be required at this point, we simply confirm that data sources are indeed what they claim to be.

Data Preparation

Data preparation involves three main mini-steps. Data cleansing, data transformation and data combination. As a whole, the data preparation step changes the raw data which was obtained from the real world to a form where it can be read and analyzed by a computer, in this case a machine learning algorithm.

First, we clean the datasets we have obtained. This is usually done by identifying missing values, errors, outliers etc. Most machine learning algorithms cannot handle missing values so it is required that they are replaced in some form or those observations associated with them be removed. For a small dataset, it is unreasonable to throw away observations, so we adopt a strategy for data imputation such as replacing missing values by averages or most occurring values (mode) for each feature. Errors from data entries may also be spotted when we notice impossible values for a particular feature example an age of 400 years. Outliers, which are data points that are so far from the observed distribution are cleaned up in this phase.

Data transformation is centered on aggregating data, dealing with categorical variables, creating dummies to ensure consistency, reducing the number of variables in order to retain the most informative features and discard redundant features, scaling the data etc. Scaling is important as features may originally be in different ranges and to get better performance, it is often sensible to bring all variables to a common range.

The data from different datasets may then be combined by merging or joining. New data views may be created depending on the type of problem, so that it is presented to the learning algorithm in a structure that is different from its original stored representation.

Data Exploration

The data exploration stage is concerned with looking closely at the data to get a better sense of what the data is all about. This step involves using statistical metrics such as mean, median, mode, variance etc to understand the data distribution. Information displayed in pictorial form is often easier to digest and as a result it is not uncommon to notice that this step includes many visualization techniques. Some common visualization techniques used in exploratory data analysis phase includes, bar charts, pie charts, histograms, line graphs, box plots etc.

Below are some common examples of visualization techniques used in this stage.

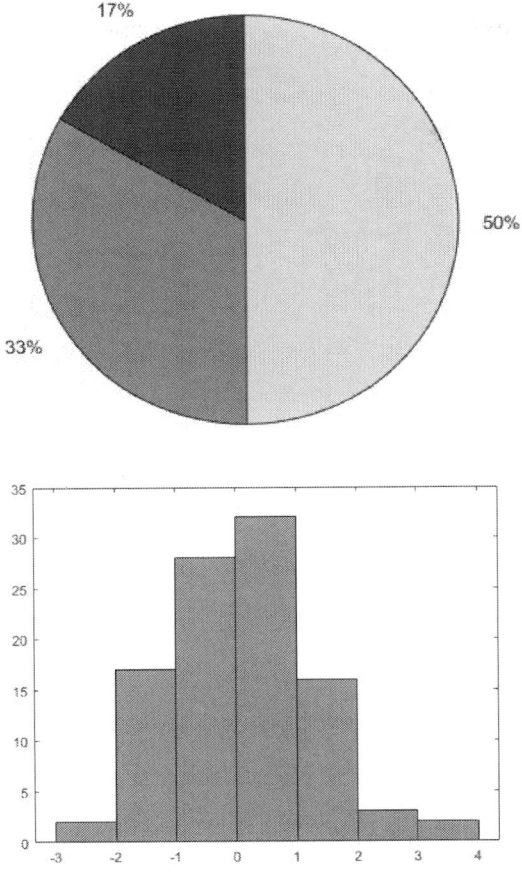

The left image is a pie chart while the image on the right is a simple histogram. The advantage of using visualization becomes obvious as we would be able to easily identify anomalies in our data and have a better mental representation of what our data contains. Sometimes anomalies in the data are noticed through exploratory data analysis and corrected by going back to the previous step - data preparation. Another important benefit of data exploration, is that it enable us discover patterns which we may combine with domain knowledge to create (engineer) new informative features.

Data Modelling

In the data modelling step we take a more involved approach when accessing the data. Data modelling involves choosing an algorithm, usually from the related fields of statistics, data mining or machine learning. Deciding which features should go into the algorithm as the input, executing the model and finally evaluating the trained model for performance.

Before feeding in data to any model, we first chose the most important features as inputs to the model. These would be features that offer the most discriminability. What that means is that we would give preference to features that contain underlying properties that enables our model learn its task better, whether that is classification or regression for example. We choose features that show the most variability across our data distribution. Those features which do not drive the final prediction or are uninformative are dropped. Techniques such as Principal Component Analysis (PCA) can be used to identify important features known as principal components. These are components along whose axes variability can be observed.

The next step involves choosing an appropriate algorithm for the learning task. Different algorithms are better suited to different learning problems. Logistic regression, Naive Bayes classifier, Support Vector Machines, decision trees and random forests are some popular classification algorithms with good performance. Linear regression and neural networks may be used for regression tasks. There are a variety of modelling algorithms and we often do not know the best algorithms before we have tried them on the dataset. It is therefore important to keep an open mind and rely heavily on experimentation.

In order to be able to support experimentation without biasing our models in the process, we adopt an evaluation scheme. Remember that the aim of modelling is to produce models that can generalize to real world data. We do not want our model to memorize the data that it was trained on. What we desire is for the model to find interesting patterns which would help it explain the structure of the data and enable it answer questions in the real world. To do this we never train our model on the entire data we have acquired and preprocessed. We divide the data into three sections known as splits. The three splits are train, validation and test sets. The train split is used for training the model while the validation split is used for hyperparameter tuning. Hyperparameter tuning means adjusting the hyperparameters (input options) available to an algorithm and checking its performance on the validation set to see whether the adjusted hyperparameter had a positive effect or not. Hyperparameter tuning is done on the most promising models to further improve performance. Finally, the trained model is evaluated on the test set which was not used for training or validation. In other words, the model has never seen the data contained in the test set. This provides an unbiased assessment of the model as we can observe its generalization to new data. The performance on the test set is normally reported as the final evaluation of the model.

The evaluation metric on the train and validation splits enable us to debug the model to discover whether it is underfitting or overfitting to the training set. If it is underfitting (not learning enough), we can increase the power of the model else we apply regularization if it is overfitting (learning noise). The concepts of overfitting and underfitting would be explained further in the next chapter.

Data Presentation

The last stage is all about presenting our findings in a form that is intuitive and understandable to non-technical professionals such as managers, marketers or business leaders. The importance of this step cannot be overemphasized as it is the crowning jewel of the data science process. Presentation is usually done by leveraging visualizations and tables. The purpose of this step is to communicate the insights discovered from the data science process in such a way that the information provided is actionable. This means data presentation should enable a decision making process. It should be clear from the presentation what steps need to be taken to solve the original problem which was posed as a question in the first step. It may also be desirable to automate the process as the insights produced may be so valuable that they need to be returned to regularly. Another possible outcome is bundling the model into a data product or application that is served to end users. To do this, the model would need to be optimized for production and deployed in a scalable fashion.

Machine Learning

What is Machine Learning

Machine learning has recently been attracting attention in the media for several reasons, mainly because it has achieved impressive results in various cognitive tasks such as image classification, natural language understanding, customer churn prediction etc. However, it has been regarded as some sort of magic formula that is capable of predicting the future, but what really is machine learning. Machine learning at its simplest form is all about making computers learn from data by improving their performance at a specific task through experience. Similar to the way humans learn by trying out new things and learning from the experience, machine learning algorithms improve their capability by learning patterns from lots of examples. The performance of these algorithms, generally improves as they are exposed to more data (experience). Machine learning is therefore a branch of artificial intelligence that aims to make machines capable of performing specific tasks without being explicitly programmed. What this means is that these algorithms are not rule-based, the entire learning process is constructed in such a way as to minimize or completely eliminate human intervention.

Machine learning algorithms are typically used for a wide range of learning problems such as classification, regression, clustering, similarity detection etc. Many applications used in the real world today are powered by machine learning. Applications such as personal assistants on mobile phones use machine learning algorithms to understand voice commands spoken in natural language, mobile keyboards predict the next word a user is typing based on previous words, email clients offer a smart reply feature whereby the content of an email is scanned and appropriate responses are generated, e-commerce applications offer recommendation to users based on previous purchases and spending habits etc. Nearly every industry would be impacted by machine learning as most processes can be automated given that there is enough training data available. Machine learning algorithms mostly excel in tasks where there is a clear relationship between a set of inputs and outputs which can be modelled by training data. Although machine learning is a rapidly improving field, there is as of now no notion of general intelligence of the form displayed by humans. This is because models trained on one task cannot generalize the knowledge gleaned to perform another task, that is machine learning algorithms learn narrow verticals of tasks.

There are three main branches of machine learning namely - supervised learning, unsupervised learning and reinforcement learning. In some cases a fourth branch is mentioned - semi-supervised learning but this is really just a special instance of supervised learning as we would see in the explanations below.

Supervised Learning Algorithms

Supervised learning is by far the most common branch of machine learning. Most of the real world value currently in the field of machine learning can be attributed to supervised learning. Supervised learning algorithms are those machine learning algorithms which are trained with labelled examples.

It would be remembered that we defined machine learning as making algorithms that learn from data (examples) without being explicitly programmed. The main intuition to understand when dealing with supervised learning algorithms is that, they learn through the use of examples that are clearly annotated to show them what they are supposed to learn. The algorithms therefore try to find a mapping representation from inputs to outputs using the labels as a guide. "Supervised" in the name of these types of algorithms, point to the fact that the labels or targets provide supervision throughout the learning process. It is therefore possible for the algorithm to check its prediction against actual values stored in the labels. It then uses this error information (how far off its prediction was from the actual label) to slowly improve its performance with each iteration. The targets in a supervised learning problem can be seen as a supervisor providing feedback to the algorithm on areas where it can improve its performance. The two main applications of supervised learning algorithms are classification and regression.

Classification involves training a learning algorithm to correctly separate examples into predefined categories or classes. The classes are usually chosen ahead of time by a human expert with domain knowledge in the field where the learning problem is posed. The examples that are used to train the model are clearly labelled to indicate the category they belong to. During training, the supervised learning algorithm, uses the labels to guide its learning and at test time it is capable of correctly predicting the categories of new examples. A popular example of classification is spam detection where an email is correctly identified to belong to one of two classes - spam or not spam. Depending on what is predicted, appropriate action could be taken such as shifting spam emails to a spam folder while relevant emails are sent to a user's inbox.

Regression is a learning problem where the algorithm is interested in predicting a single real value number. Regression is used where a single numeric entity is to be predicted. An example of regression would be predicting the age of a person given a profile picture or predicting the salary of an individual given information about the individual such as level of education, work experience, age, country of residence etc. It would be observed that in both cases the final prediction is a single number.

Supervised learning algorithms are easier to train when compared to unsupervised or reinforcement learning algorithms. This is because the presence of labels simplify the learning problem since there exist a clear way of determining performance during training. However, it should be noted that most supervised learning problems can also be modelled as unsupervised if we get rid of labels. Datasets for supervised learning are more expensive to acquire as it requires meticulous human annotation of examples. The fact that most data in the world today are in an unlabelled form makes the research of unsupervised learning algorithms particularly important.

Unsupervised Learning Algorithms

Unsupervised learning involves learning directly from raw data. This type of learning takes place without the presence of a supervisor in the training loop in form of labels. Unsupervised learning algorithms are free to explore the underlying data distribution and come up with patterns that best describe the entire dataset. The training process is not guided by humans through labelled examples and as such unsupervised learning algorithms are more powerful as they can discover patterns which domain experts may not have thought of. It is however still the job of domain experts to understand the patterns so discovered and explain them because unsupervised learning algorithms do not truly have the sense of reasoning which we would ascribe to humans. Unsupervised learning algorithms merely use the data distribution or its latent (hidden) representations to unearth insights which may be in the form clusters, groups or distributions.

There are many applications of unsupervised learning algorithms such as clustering, dimensionality detection, generative models etc. Clustering is one of the popular implementations of unsupervised learning. It involves the automatic discovery of groups (clusters) of data points from raw data. Members of a group share similar features, that is they are alike. They can be thought of as belonging to the same type of entity whereas as a group they are dissimilar to other groups. Groups usually have semantic meaning which can be further explored to understand the dataset. An example of clustering would involve grouping customers of a tv streaming service into the type of shows that they watch. Users with similar interests would generally be found in the same group. This is a very powerful application as new tv shows could be recommended to users based on other users who share their interests, leading to greater engagement on the platform and increased revenues.

Dimensionality reduction is a machine learning technique that reduces the number of attributes (features) fed in a model to only the most relevant ones which drive predictions. It has been observed empirically, that models with greater number of features or dimensions perform worse on generalization. That is to say that their performance suffers in the real world. By reducing the number of dimensions, a model can learn from informative features which enables it to develop valid representations about the data that aids prediction. Principal component Analysis (PCA) is probably the most popular dimensionality reduction technique and is an example of an unsupervised learning algorithm. PCA reduces the dimensions of data by identifying those axes that contain the most variability. What that means is that it discovers principal components which offer the most discriminative features.

Generative models are another popular instance of unsupervised learning algorithms. They have made recent headlines because of their ability to artificially generate photographs and works of art that look realistic. Generative Adversarial Networks (GANs) currently produce state of the art results across many image generation benchmarks and are among the most popular examples of generative models.

Semi-supervised Learning Algorithms

Semi-supervised learning algorithms are a special case of supervised learning algorithms. In semi-supervised learning, while there isn't an explicit label, there exist an implicit heuristic which serves as a supervisor in the training loop.

Semi-supervised models do not contain any external source of labels but only rely on input features. However, the learning task is set up in such a way that supervision still takes place in the form of extraction of pseudo-labels from inputs through a heuristic algorithm. A popular example of semi-supervised learning algorithms are autoencoders. Let us look at an example to expand our understanding.

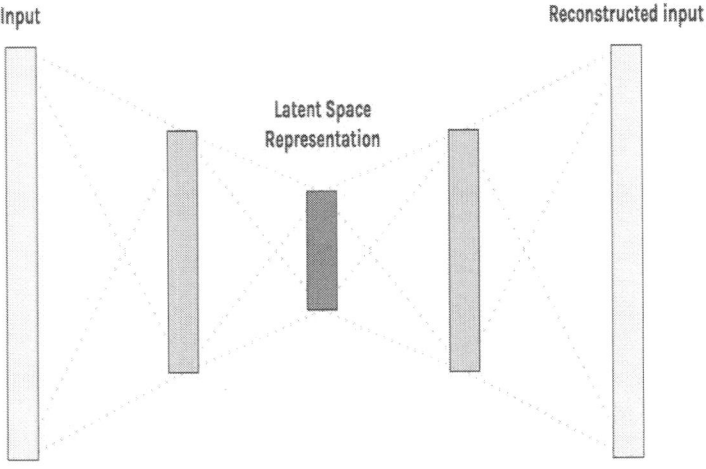

In the autoencoder above, the learning task is to reduce the dimensions of the input into a smaller latent space representing the most important hidden features, then reconstruct the input from this lower dimensional space. So given an input, example an image, an autoencoder shrinks the image into a smaller latent representation that still contains most of the information about the image, then reconstructs the original input image from this low dimensional space. Even if there are no explicit labels, it would be observed that the input serves as the supervisor since the learning task is to reconstruct the input. Once such a model is trained to compress features into a smaller dimension, the compressed features can serve as the starting point of a supervised learning algorithm similar to dimensionality reduction using PCA. The first part of the network that reduces the dimensions of the input is called an encoder while the second part that scales the encoded features back to the full size input is called the decoder.

Reinforcement Learning Algorithms

In reinforcement learning there are three main components, an agent, an environment and actions. The goal of reinforcement learning is to train an intelligent agent that is capable of navigating its environment and performing actions that maximizes its chances of arriving at some end goal. Actions carried out by the agent change the state of the environment and rewards or punishment may be issued based on the actions taken by the agent. The challenge is for the agent to maximize the accumulated rewards at the end of a specific period so that it can actualize an end goal (objective).

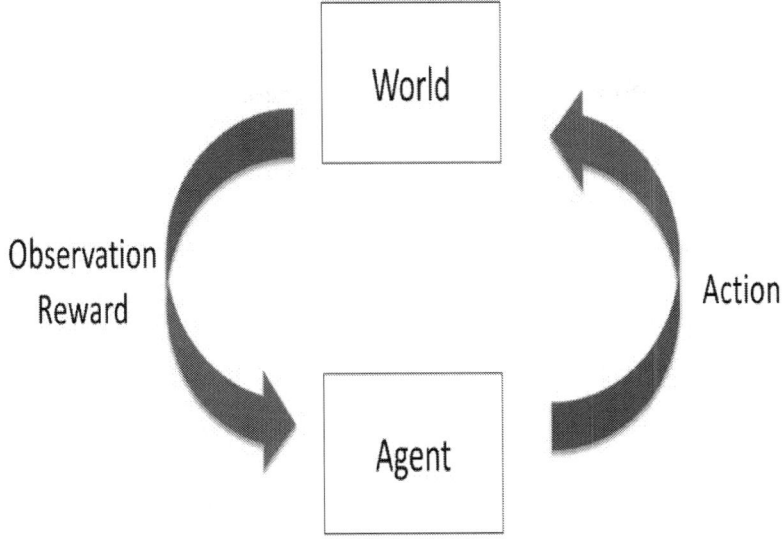

In the schematic diagram of reinforcement learning above, an agent (the reinforcement learning) interacts with the world (environment) through actions. The environment provides observations and rewards to the agent based on the kind of action taken by the agent. The agent uses this feedback to improve its decision making process by learning to carry out actions associated with positive outcomes.

Overfitting and Underfitting

Overfitting and underfitting jointly form the central problem of machine learning. When training a model we want to improve its optimization by attaining better performance on the training set. However, once the model is trained, what we care about is generalization. Generalization in a nutshell deals with how well a trained machine learning model would perform on new data which it has not seen, that is data it was not trained on. In other words, how well can a model generalize the patterns it learnt on the training set to suit real world examples, so that it can achieve similar or better performance. This is the crux of learning. A model should be able to actually learn useful representations from data that improves test time performance and not merely memorize features as memorization is not learning.

We say a model has overfit to a training set when it has failed to learn only useful representations in the data but has also adjusted itself to learn noise in order to get an artificially high training set accuracy. Underfitting means that the model has not used the information available to it but has only learnt a small subset of representations and has thrown away majority of useful information, thereby making it to make unfounded assumptions. The ideal situation is to find a model that neither underfitts nor overfitts but exhibits the right balance between optimization and generalization. This can be done by maintaining a third set of examples known as the validation set. The validation set is used to tune (improve) the performance of the model without overfitting the model to the training set. Other techniques for tackling overfitting includes applying regularization which punishes more complicated models and acquiring more training examples. Underfitting can be stymied by increasing the capacity of the learning algorithm so that it can take advantage of available features.

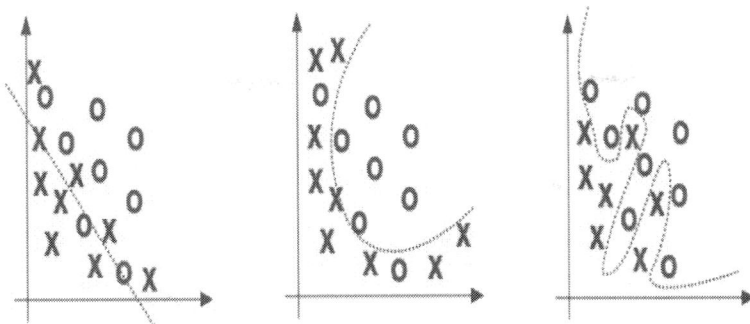

The plots above show three simple line based classification models. The first plot separates classes by using a straight line. However, a straight line is an overly simplistic representation for the data distribution and as a result it misclassified many examples. The straight line model is clearly underfitting as it has failed to use majority of the information available to it to discover the inherent data distribution.

The second plot shows an optimal case where the optimization objective has been balanced by generalization criterion. Even though the model misclassified some points in the training set, it was still able to capture a valid decision boundary between both classes. Such a classifier is likely to generalize well to examples which it was not trained on as it has learnt the discriminative features that drive prediction. The last plot illustrates a case of overfitting. The decision boundary is convoluted because the classifier is responding to noise by trying to correctly classify every data point in the training set. The accuracy of this classifier would be perfect on the training set but it would perform horribly on new examples because it optimized its performance only for the training set. The trick is to always choose the simplest model that achieves the greatest performance.

Correctness

To evaluate a machine learning algorithm, we always specific measures of predictive performance. These metrics allow us to judge the performance of a model in an unbiased fashion. It should be noted that the evaluation metric chosen depends on the type of learning problem. Accuracy is a popular evaluation metric but it is not suitable for all learning problems. Other measures for evaluation include recall, precision, sensitivity, specificity, true positive rate, false positive rate etc. The evaluation used should be in line with the goals of the modelling problem.

To ensure fidelity of reported metrics, a rule of thumb is that models should never be trained on the entire dataset as any evaluation reported by metrics is likely skewed because the model's performance when exposed to new data is unascertained. The dataset should be divided into train, validation and test splits. The model is trained on the training set, the validation set is reserved for hyperparameter tuning for best performing models and the test set is only used once at the conclusion of all experimentation.

A confusion matrix is widely used as a simple visualization technique to access the performance of classifiers in a supervised learning task. It is a table where the rows represent the instances in the actual class (ground truth) while the columns represents predictions. The order may be reversed in some cases. It is called a confusion matrix because it makes it easy to see which classes the model is misclassifying for another, that is which classes confuse the model.

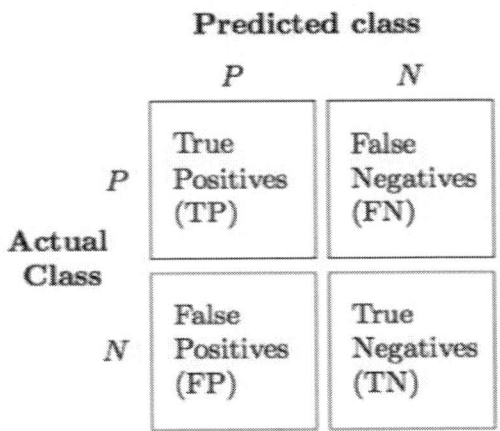

The examples which the model correctly classified are on the diagonal from the top left to bottom right. False negatives are positive classes which the classified wrongly predicted as negatives while false positives are negative instances which the classifier wrongly thought were positives. Several metrics like true positive rate, false positive rate, precision etc are derived from items in the confusion matrix.

The Bias-Variance Trade-off

The bias of a model is defined as the assumptions made by the model to simplify the learning task. A model with high bias makes assumptions which are not correlated by the data. This lead to errors because predictions are usually some way off from actuals. Variance on the other hand is how susceptible a model is to noise in the training data. How widely does the performance on the model vary based on the data it is evaluated on. A good machine learning algorithm should strive to achieve low bias and low variance. Bias and variance are related to overfitting and underfitting earlier encountered. A model with high bias is underfitting the training data because it has made simplistic assumptions instead of learning from information available. Similarly, a model with high variance is overfitting, because it has modelled noise and as a result, its performance would vary widely across the training set, validation set and test set.

Let us look use a dart analogy to further explain these concepts.

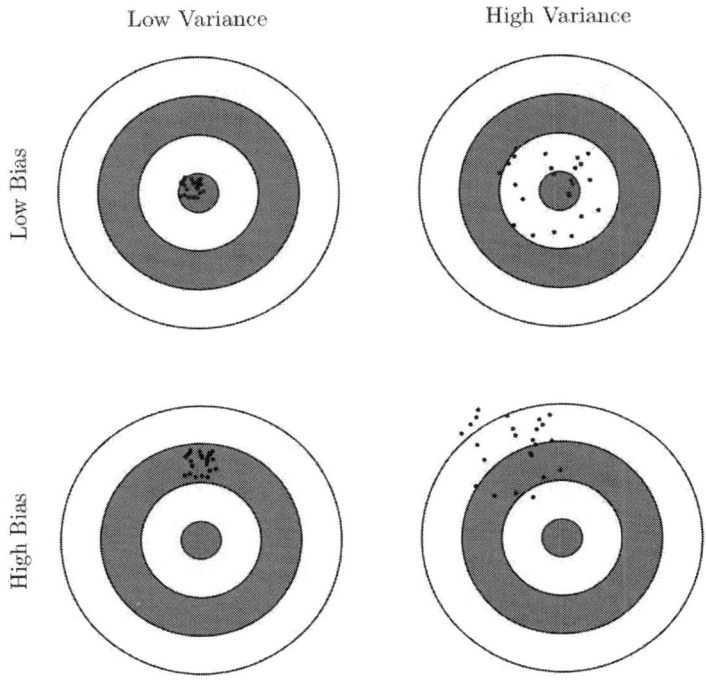

Low Variance   High Variance

Low Bias

High Bias

The top left image represents a model that has low bias and low variance. This is the ideal model as it has learnt to hit the target (produce correct classification) and usually hits the target most of the time (does not vary with each throw). The image at the top right shows a model that exhibits high variance and low bias. Even if it does not make a lot of assumptions, its predictions are spread all over the board which means its performance varies widely (high variance). The image on the bottom left depicts a model with high bias and low variance. The shots are not all over the board but in a specific location. This location is however far from the target meaning the model is biased because of simplistic assumptions. Finally, the image on the bottom right shows a model with high bias and high variance. The shots on the board vary widely and are far away from the target. This is the worst kind of model as it hasn't learnt any useful representation.

Feature Extraction and Selection

Feature extraction involves performing transformation on input features that produce other features that are more analyzable and informative. Feature extraction may occur by combining original features to create new features which are better suited for the modelling problem. This is similar to feature engineering where we create new features to fed into a model. An example of feature extraction is Principal Component Analysis (PCA).

Feature selection is choosing a subset of features from the original input features. The features selected are those that show the most correlation with the target variable, that is those features that drive the predictive capability of the model. Both feature extraction and feature selection leads to dimensionality reduction. The main difference between them is that feature extraction is a transformation that creates new features whereas feature selection chooses only a subset of available features. Since feature selection removes certain features, it is always advisable to first do feature extraction on a dataset, then select the most important predictors via feature selection.

Overview of Python Programming Language

The Python Programming Language

Python is a general purpose programming language language used in web development, scientific computing, system administration, software development etc. Python favors readability and has an English like syntax. One of the main differences between Python and other programming languages like Java, C++, PHP etc is that it does not make use of curly braces to define scope. Blocks of code, called suites in Python are delineated using whitespace. Python is also a dynamically typed language which means variable types do not have to be declared before variables are used. It makes use of duck typing which makes certain assumptions about the type of a variable from its content. Duck typing in programming is coined from the popular phrase - "If it walks like a duck and quacks like a duck, then it's a duck". What this means in essence is that if an object exhibits certain properties, then its type can be deduced. This is a powerful assumption as it allows code to be written interactively and defers type checking to when the program is actually run (runtime).

Python is a very expressive programming language and is favored by programmers and scientists because it encourages quick prototyping and significantly reduces development time when compared to other high level programming languages. In data science, Python enables fast iteration of data science projects and because Python is a general purpose programming language, prototype models can be more easily integrated into production workflows as there is usually no need to switch to another programming language. In this way, one language can be used for the entire stack, from prototyping to deployment. It should be noted however, that this generally depends on the type of application and Python especially for scientific computing usually reference lower level extensions in faster programming languages like C or C++. Python can be seen as the ideal interface to work across a slew of tasks effectively and efficiently.

Python was created by Guido van Rossum in 1991 and has undergone several iterations. There are currently two major versions of Python - Python 2 and Python 3. At the time of this writing the development of Python 2 has been discontinued so it is advised to use Python 3 for all new projects. For this reason, the examples we would come across in this book all assume a Python 3 environment.

There are several ways to set up a local Python development environment such as installing Python natively on a computer, setting up a virtual environment using a tool like virtualenv or using a bundled scientific distribution like Anaconda. For the purposes of this book, we would leverage the immensely popular scientific distribution Anaconda because it contains many prepackaged Python scientific libraries, some of which we would use throughout this book. Anaconda is cross platform and is available for the major operating systems - Windows, Linux, macOS etc. You can download the Anaconda installer for your operating system by going to their download page (https://www.anaconda.com/downloads) and following the installation instructions.

Once Anaconda has been installed on your computer, new Python packages can be installed by using Anaconda's package manager, "conda" or using Python's native package manager - "pip". It should also be noted that packages should be upgraded or deleted using the appropriate package manager through which the package was installed.

Here are examples instructions on installing packages from the terminal for both cases:

$ **conda install package_name** # installation via conda package manager

$ **pip install package_name** # installation via pip

Similarly, an installed package can be updated using the following commands.

$ **conda update package_name** # update via conda package manager

$ **pip install --upgrade package_name** # upgrade via pip

Common Python Syntax

In this section, a brief overview of basic Python syntax is presented. As would become evident, indentation is important as all lines of code in the same suite (block) must be indented by an equal number of characters. By convention, this is usually

4 white spaces. Let us honour traditions and start with a simple Hello world! example in Python.

```
print('Hello World!')
```

The code above outputs the string "Hello World!" to the screen.

Next, we look at variable assignment. Variables can be seen as containers that point to an entity or stored value. Entities are assigned to a variable using the equality operator. The value on the right hand side is put into the container on the left hand side. A variable usually has a name and calling the variable by its name references the stored object.

```
a = 3
b = 4
c = a + b
print('The value of a is {}, while the value of b is {}, and
their sum c is {}'.format(a, b, c))
```

```
The value of a is 3, while the value of b is 4, and their sum c is 7
```

The code above assigns an integer with a value of 3 to the variable named **a**, it also assigns 4 to **b** and finally computes the sum of **a** and **b** and stores it in a new variable **c**. It should be noted from the above piece of code that we never explicitly defined the types of variables we created, rather the type information was gotten from the kind of entity the object contained. There are mainly types of mathematical operations available in Python apart from addition used above. A good approach is to familiarize yourself with the Python documentation as the standard Python library contains many useful utilities. The documentation for Python 3 can be accessed at https://docs.python.org/3.

Moving forward, Python supports the use of conditionals to determine which suite of code to execute. Regular conditionals such as if, else if and else are available in Python. One thing to note is that else if is expressed as elif in Python. Let us look at a simple example below.

```python
a = 200
b = 33
if b > a:
   print("b is greater than a")
elif a == b:
   print("a and b are equal")
else:
   print("a is greater than b")
```

```
a is greater than b
```

The code snippet above uses conditionals to determine which suite of code to run. Suites use whitespace indentation for separation and the output printed to the screen is determined by the evaluation of the conditional in line with the declared variables contained therein.

Another important Python syntax are loops. Loops are used for repeating a block of code several times. They may be used in conjunction with conditionals.

```
for x in range(2):
  print(x)
```

The code above prints 0 and 1 to the screen. Python indexes start from 0 and the range function in Python is non inclusive. What that means is that the last value of a range is not included when it is evaluated. Loops are a very useful construct in Python and generally are in the form shown above. There is also another form known as while loops but for loops are used more often.

This brings us to the concept of a function. A function is a block of code which has been wrapped together and performs a specific task. A function is usually named but may be anonymous. In Python, a function is the major way we write reusable chunks of code. Let us look at a simple function below.

```
def my_function(planet):
```

```
print('Hello ' + planet)
```

A function is defined using the special keyword def. A function may accept arguments or return a value. To call a function (execute it), we type the function name followed by a parenthesis containing parameters if the function expects arguments, else we call it with empty parentheses.

```
my_function('Earth!')
```

```
Hello Earth!
```

Comments in Python are ignored by the interpreter and can be used to explain code or for internal documentation. There are two types of comments in Python. The first uses the pound or hash symbol which the second is known as a docstring and uses 3 quotation marks.

```
# a single line comment using pound or hash symbol
'''
A multi-line

comment in Python
'''
print('Comments in Python!')
```

Python Data Structures

Data structures are how data is collectively stored for easy access and manipulation. There are several data structures in Python which enables quick prototyping. Data structures are the format in which data is stored and usually includes the kinds of operations or functions that can be called on the data. The most popular data structure in Python are lists. Lists can contain different types of data and are ordinal. Lists are synonymous to arrays in other programming languages. Other data structures includes a tuple which is a collection that cannot be modified, a set, which is an immutable list with unique values and a dictionary, which is a key-value pair data structure. Let us look at how to create each of them below.

```
my_list = ['apple', 'banana', 4, 20]
print(my_list)
```

```
['apple', 'banana', 4, 20]
```

Lists can also be defined using the list constructor as shown below.

```
another_list = list(('a', 'b', 'c'))
print(another_list)
```

```
['a', 'b', 'c']
```

Tuples are immutable, this means that we cannot change the values of a tuple, trying to do so would result in an error. Below is how tuples are created.

```
my_tuple = (1, 2, 3, 4)
print(my_tuple)
print(type(my_tuple))
```

```
(1, 2, 3, 4)
<class 'tuple'>
```

Using the inbuilt type function gives us the type of an object.

Sets are unordered collections that can contain only unique values. Sets are created using curly braces as shown below.

```
my_set = {1, 1, 2, 2, 2, 'three'}
print(my_set)
print(type(my_set))
```

```
{'three', 1, 2}
<class 'set'>
```

In the example above, notice that all duplicate entries are removed when the set is created and there is no concept of ordering.

A dictionary is a collection of key value pairs that are unordered and can be changed. Dictionaries are created using curly braces with each key pointing to its corresponding value.

```
my_dict = {'1': 'one', '2': 'two', '3': 'three'}
print(my_dict)
print(type(my_dict))
```

```
{'1': 'one', '2': 'two', '3': 'three'}
<class 'dict'>
```

There are other data types in Python but these are by far the most commonly used ones. To understand more about these data structures and which operations that can be performed on them, read through the official Python documentation.

Python for Scientific Computing

One of the reasons for the rapid adoption of Python by the scientific community is because of the availability of scientific computing packages and the relative ease of use as most scientists are not professional programmers. This has in turn lead to better algorithms being implemented in many Python scientific packages as the community has evolved to support several packages. Another reason for the widespread adoption of Python in data science and in the larger scientific community is because Python is a well designed language and is useful across several tasks, so users do not need to learn a new programming language when confronted with a new task but can rather leverage Python's rich ecosystem of libraries to perform their tasks. Python is also easy to pick up so users can learn to extend libraries to support the functionality that they desire. This forms a virtuous cycle as libraries become more mature and support a wider range of adopters.

Scipy, also known as scientific python contains several packages that build on each other to provide a rich repository of scientific tools. Numpy or numerical Python enables numerical computation like matrix operations, Fourier transforms, random number operations etc. The Scipy library contains modules that can be used for signal processing, optimization, statistics etc, while matplotlib provides access to a powerful plotting package that can be used to produce high quality 2-dimensional and 3-dimensional plots. Other libraries in the wider ecosystem are Pandas, Scikit-Learn, Jupyter notebooks etc. We would look at each of these package in more depth in the next section.

Python Data Science Tools

Jupyter Notebook

Data science is an experimental endeavour as hypothesis needs to be tested out to see whether the data upholds them. Jupyter notebook is an interactive web application that bundles an IPython shell, which is an enhanced shell for Python computations. Code, text and visualizations can be written alongside each other and stored in a special notebook format. This means that projects can be shared easily across teams and code can be easily reproduced as every functionality that is required to execute a project is bundled in the notebook. Jupyter notebooks supports many programming languages like R, Julia, Python etc. Jupyter in Python are powered by the IPython shell which provides additional "magic" functions that are not available in Python but are generally useful for interactive computation.

Jupyter notebooks also supports Latex and as a result mathematical equations can be written inline in cell blocks. Data visualization is also possible inline and detailed documentation or explanations can be incorporated in a notebook by using markdown syntax.

IPython and Jupyter notebook are automatically installed with Anaconda. To access the Jupyter notebook interface run the following command from a terminal.

```
$ jupyter notebook # command to launch jupyter notebook web
interface
```

The command above, opens a window in a browser session containing the Jupyter notebook web interface. The Jupyter notebook session is opened in the same directory where the command is run.

You can navigate to a notebook file and click on it to run it or a create a new notebook from the interface.

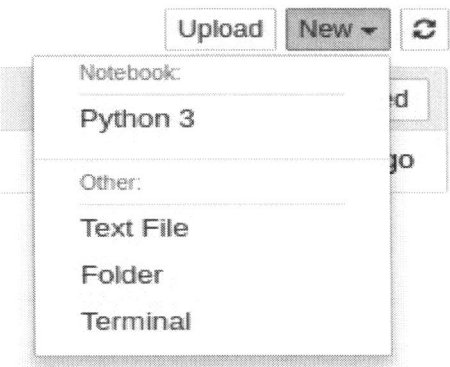

Once a new notebook is created, it launches a new instance from which coding can be carried out interactively.

```
I'm a markdown cell.

In [2]:  print("I'm a code cell")

         I'm a code cell

         I'm a **raw** cell
```

Jupyter notebooks are very popular in the fields of data science and machine learning as they offer a specialized format that encapsulates coding, visualization and documentation.

Numerical Python (Numpy)

Numpy is the main numerical computing library in Python. It provides access to a multidimensional array object and exposes several methods through which operations can be done on these arrays. It features support for linear algebra operations such as matrix multiplication, inner product, identity operations etc. Numpy interfaces with low level libraries written in C and Fortran and passes off actual computation to these faster and more efficient libraries. As a result, vanilla Python control structures like loops are never used when performing numerical computation because they are significantly slower. Numpy can be seen as providing a set of Python APIs which enables efficient scientific computing.

Numpy arrays can be initiated by nested Python lists. The level of nesting specifies the rank of the array.

```
import numpy as np

a = np.array([[1, 2, 3], [4, 5, 6]])   # create a rank 2 array
print(type(a))
print(a.shape)
```

```
<class 'numpy.ndarray'>
(2, 3)
```

The array created is of rank 2 which means that it is a matrix. We can see this clearly from the size of the array printed. It contains 2 rows and 3 columns hence size (m, n).

Arrays can also be initialized randomly from a distribution such as the normal distribution. Trainable parameters of a model such as the weights are usually initialized randomly.

```
b = np.random.random((2,2))  # create an array filled with random values
print(b)
print(b.shape)
```

```
[[ 0.46787717  0.44171202]
 [ 0.99306866  0.29371927]]
(2, 2)
```

Numpy contains many methods for manipulation of arrays, one of such is matrix product. Let us look at an example of matrix product using Numpy.

```
[[19 22]
 [43 50]]
```

```
x = np.array([[1, 2], [3, 4]])
y = np.array([[5, 6], [7, 8]])

# matrix product
print(np.dot(x, y))
```

The example above is computed almost instantly and shows the power of Numpy.

Pandas

Pandas is a data manipulation library written in Python which features high performance data structures for table and time series data. Pandas is used extensively for data analysis and most data loading, cleaning and transformation tasks are performed in Pandas. Pandas is an integral part of the Python data science ecosystem as data is rarely in a form that can be fed directly into machine learning models. Data from the real world is usually messy, contains missing values and in need of transformation. Pandas supports many file types like CSV, Excel spreadsheets, Python pickle format, JSON, SQL etc.

There are two main types of Pandas data structures - series and dataframe. Series is the data structure for a single column of data while a dataframe stores 2-dimensional data analogous to a matrix. In other words, a dataframe contains data stored in many columns.

The code below shows how to create a Series object in Pandas.

```
import pandas as pd

s = pd.Series([1, 3, 5, np.nan, 6, 8])

print(s)
```

To create a dataframe, we can run the following code.

```
df = pd.DataFrame(np.random.randn(6, 4), columns=list('ABCD'))

print(df)
```

Pandas loads the file formats it supports into a dataframe and manipulation on the dataframe can then occur using Pandas methods.

Scientific Python (Scipy)

Scipy is a scientific computing library geared towards the fields of mathematics, science and engineering. It is built on top of

Numpy and extends it by providing additional modules for optimization, technical computing, statistics, signal processing etc. Scipy is mostly used in conjunction with other tools in the ecosystem like Pandas and matplotlib.

Here is a simple usage of scipy that finds the inverse of a matrix.

```
from scipy import linalg
z = np.array([[1, 2], [3, 4]])

print(linalg.inv(z))
```

```
[[-2.   1. ]
 [ 1.5 -0.5]]
```

Matplotlib

Matplotlib is a plotting library that integrates nicely with Numpy and other numerical computation libraries in Python. It is capable of producing quality plots and is widely used in data exploration where visualization techniques are important. Matplotlib exposes an object oriented API making it easy to create powerful visualizations in Python. Note that to see the plot in Jupyter notebooks you must use the matplotlib inline magic command.

Here is an example that uses Matplotlib to plot a sine waveform.

```
# magic command for Jupyter notebooks
%matplotlib inline

import matplotlib.pyplot as plt

# compute the x and y coordinates for points on a sine curve
x = np.arange(0, 3 * np.pi, 0.1)
y = np.sin(x)

# plot the points using matplotlib
plt.plot(x, y)
plt.show()  # Show plot by calling plt.show()
```

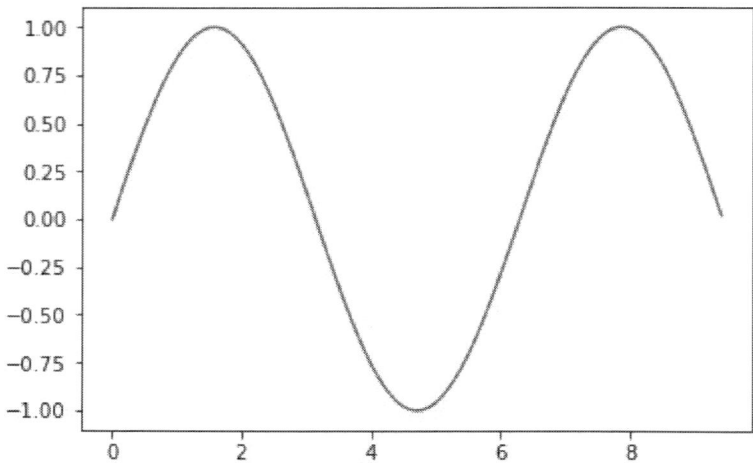

Scikit-Learn

Scikit-Learn is the most popular machine learning library in the Python ecosystem. It is a very mature library and contains several algorithms for classification, regression and clustering. Many common algorithms are available in Scikit-Learn and it exposes a consistent interface to access them, therefore learning how to work with one classifier in Scikit-Learn means that you would be able to work with others as the names of the methods that are called to train a classifier are the same regardless of the underlying implementation.

We would rely heavily on Scikit-Learn for our modelling tasks as we dive deeper into data science in the following sections of this book. Here is a simple example of creating a classifier and training it on one of the bundled datasets.

```
# sample decision tree classifier
```

```
from sklearn import datasets
from sklearn import metrics
from sklearn.tree import DecisionTreeClassifier

# load the iris datasets
dataset = datasets.load_iris()

# fit a CART model to the data
model = DecisionTreeClassifier()
model.fit(dataset.data, dataset.target)
print(model)

# make predictions
expected = dataset.target
predicted = model.predict(dataset.data)

# summarize the fit of the model
print(metrics.classification_report(expected, predicted))
print(metrics.confusion_matrix(expected, predicted))
```

Here is the output. Do not worry if you do not understand the code. We would go through each part of the code in more detail in subsequent sections.

```
DecisionTreeClassifier(class_weight=None, criterion='gini', max_depth=None,
        max_features=None, max_leaf_nodes=None,
        min_impurity_decrease=0.0, min_impurity_split=None,
        min_samples_leaf=1, min_samples_split=2,
        min_weight_fraction_leaf=0.0, presort=False, random_state=None,
        splitter='best')
             precision    recall  f1-score   support

          0       1.00      1.00      1.00        50
          1       1.00      1.00      1.00        50
          2       1.00      1.00      1.00        50

avg / total       1.00      1.00      1.00       150

[[50  0  0]
 [ 0 50  0]
 [ 0  0 50]]
```

K-Nearest Neighbors

Handling Data

The K-Nearest Neighbor algorithm is an instance based machine learning algorithm that can be used for classification and regression although it is mainly used for the former. KNN is a non-parametric algorithm, what that means is that there are no parameters to be learnt by the model. As we would see in this section, K-nearest Neighbor algorithm is easy to understand and implement. At the core of the algorithm is a distance metric which calculates the similarity between samples and infers the class of a test sample from its closest neighbor hence the name K-Nearest neighbor. K refers to the number of samples to consider when arriving at a final prediction for a test instance. If k is 5, then the 5 closest neighbors to that sample are considered and the predicted class would be the majority class from the votes from those five neighbors. Such a case would be referred to as 5-Nearest Neighbors. If only the closest neighbor according to the distance metric is considered k-NN becomes Nearest Neighbor algorithm and the class of the closest sample to a test instance is returned as the class of that test sample.

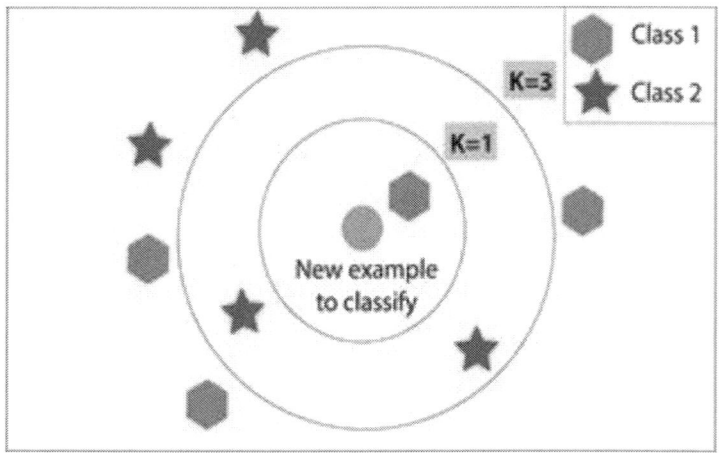

In the image above, when k = 1, the class of the test point is predicted to be class 1 (blue diamond), which is the class of the closest sample to it. When k = 3, a vote is taken amongst the 3 closest classes and the majority vote is chosen as the predicted class, in this case class 2 (red star).

Now that we have a good understanding of the algorithm, let us implement it from scratch in Python and test it on a dataset. The dataset we would use for this task is the Iris flower classification dataset. The dataset contains 150 examples of 3 classes of species of Iris flowers namely Iris Setosa, Iris Versicolor and Iris Virginica. The dataset can be downloaded from Kaggle (https://www.kaggle.com/saurabh00007/iriscsv/downloads/Iris.csv/1).

The first step of the data science process is to acquire data, which we have done. Next we need to handle the data or preprocess it into a suitable form before passing it off to a machine learning classifier.

To begin let's import all relevant libraries.

```
import numpy as np
import pandas as pd
import matplotlib.pyplot as plt
import scipy as sp
```

Next we use Pandas to load the dataset which is contained in a CSV file and print out the first few rows so that we can have a sense of what is contained in the dataset.

```
dataset = pd.read_csv('Iris.csv')
dataset.head(5)
```

Id	SepalLengthCm	SepalWidthCm	PetalLengthCm	PetalWidthCm	Species
0	1	5.1	3.5	1.4	0.2 Iris-setosa
1	2	4.9	3.0	1.4	0.2 Iris-setosa
2	3	4.7	3.2	1.3	0.2 Iris-setosa
3	4	4.6	3.1	1.5	0.2 Iris-setosa
4	5	5.0	3.6	1.4	0.2 Iris-setosa

As we can see, there are 4 predictors namely sepal length, sepal width, petal length and petal width. Species is the target variable that we are interested in predicting. Since there are 3 classes what we have is a multi-classification problem.

In line with our observations, we separate the columns into features (X) and targets (y).

```
X = dataset.iloc[:, 1:5].values # select features ignoring non-
informative column Id

y = dataset.iloc[:, 5].values # Species contains targets for our
model
```

Our targets are currently stored as text. We need to transform them into categorical variables. To do this we leverage Scikit-Learn label encoder.

```
from sklearn.preprocessing import LabelEncoder
```

```
le = LabelEncoder()

y = le.fit_transform(y)  # transform species names into
categorical values
```

Next we split our dataset into a training set and a test set so that we can evaluate the performance of our trained model appropriately.

```
from sklearn.model_selection import train_test_split

X_train, X_test, y_train, y_test = train_test_split(X, y,
test_size = 0.3)
```

Calculating Similarity

In the last section, we successfully prepared our data and explained the inner workings of the K-NN algorithm at a high level. We would now implement a working version in Python. The most important part of K-NN algorithm is the similarity metric which in this case is a distance measure. There are several distance metrics but we would use Euclidean distance which is the straight line distance between two points in a Euclidean plane. The plane may be 2-dimensional, 3-dimensional etc. Euclidean distance is sometimes referred to as L2 distance. It is given by the formula below.

$$d(\mathbf{p}, \mathbf{q}) = d(\mathbf{q}, \mathbf{p}) = \sqrt{(q_1 - p_1)^2 + (q_2 - p_2)^2 + \cdots + (q_n - p_n)^2}$$

$$= \sqrt{\sum_{i=1}^{n} (q_i - p_i)^2}.$$

The L2 distance is computed from the test sample to every sample in the training set to determine how close they are. We can implement L2 distance in Python using Numpy as shown below.

```
def euclidean_distance(training_set, test_instance):
    # number of samples inside training set
    n_samples = training_set.shape[0]

    # create array for distances
    distances = np.empty(n_samples, dtype=np.float64)

    # euclidean distance calculation
    for i in range(n_samples):
        distances[i] = np.sqrt(np.sum(np.square(test_instance -
training_set[i])))


    return distances
```

Locating Neighbors

Having implemented the similarity metric, we can build out a full fledged class that is capable of identifying nearest neighbors and returning a classification. It should be noted that the K-Nearest Neighbor algorithm has no training phase. It simply stores all data points in memory. It only performs computation during test time when it is calculating distances and returning predictions. Here is an implementation of the K-NN algorithm that utilizes the distance function defined above.

```python
class MyKNeighborsClassifier():
    """

    Vanilla implementation of KNN algorithm.
    """


    def __init__(self, n_neighbors=5):
        self.n_neighbors=n_neighbors


    def fit(self, X, y):
        """

        Fit the model using X as array of features and y as array
of labels.
        """

        n_samples = X.shape[0]
        # number of neighbors can't be larger then number of
samples
```

```
        if self.n_neighbors > n_samples:

                raise ValueError("Number of neighbors can't be larger
then number of samples in training set.")


        # X and y need to have the same number of samples
        if X.shape[0] != y.shape[0]:

                raise ValueError("Number of samples in X and y need
to be equal.")


        # finding and saving all possible class labels
        self.classes_ = np.unique(y)


        self.X = X
        self.y = y


    def    pred_from_neighbors(self,    training_set,    labels,
test_instance, k):
        distances       =        euclidean_distance(training_set,
test_instance)


        # combining arrays as columns
        distances = sp.c_[distances, labels]
        # sorting array by value of first column
        sorted_distances = distances[distances[:,0].argsort()]
        # selecting labels associeted with k smallest distances
        targets = sorted_distances[0:k,1]
```

```python
        unique, counts = np.unique(targets, return_counts=True)
        return(unique[np.argmax(counts)])



    def predict(self, X_test):

        # number of predictions to make and number of features
inside single sample
        n_predictions, n_features = X_test.shape

        # allocationg space for array of predictions
        predictions = np.empty(n_predictions, dtype=int)

        # loop over all observations
        for i in range(n_predictions):
            # calculation of single prediction
            predictions[i]  =  self.pred_from_neighbors(self.X,
self.y, X_test[i, :], self.n_neighbors)


        return(predictions)
```

The workflow of the class above is that during test time, a test
sample (instance) is supplied and the Euclidean distance to
every sample in the entire training set is calculated. Depending
on the value of nearest neighbors to consider, the labels of
those neighbors participate in a vote to determine the class of
the test sample.

Generating Response

In order to generate a response or create a prediction, we first have to initialize our custom classifier. The value of k, cannot exceed the number of samples in our dataset. This is to be expected because we cannot compare with a greater number of neighbors than what we have available in the training set.

```
# instantiate learning model  (k = 3)
my_classifier = MyKNeighborsClassifier(n_neighbors=3)
```

Next we can train our model on the data. Remember in K-NN no training actually takes place.

```
# fitting the model
my_classifier.fit(X_train, y_train)
```

Evaluating Accuracy

To evaluate the accuracy of our model, we test its performance on examples which it has not seen such as those contained in the test set.

```
# predicting the test set results
my_y_pred = my_classifier.predict(X_test)
```

We then check the predicted classes against the ground truth labels and use Scikit-Learn accuracy module to calculate the accuracy of our classifier.

```
from sklearn.metrics import confusion_matrix, accuracy_score
accuracy = accuracy_score(y_test, my_y_pred)*100
print('Accuracy: ' + str(round(accuracy, 2)) + ' %.')
```

Accuracy: 97.78 %.

Our model achieves an accuracy of 97.8% which is impressive for such a simple and elegant model.

The Curse of Dimensionality

The K-Nearest Neighbor algorithm performs optimally when the dimension of the input space is small as in this example. We had four predictors (sepal length, sepal width, petal length, petal width) going into the algorithm. K-NN struggles in high dimensional input spaces like those encountered in images. This is because the similarity measure as expressed by the distance metric is very limited and cannot properly model this high dimensional space. In general, machine learning algorithms try to reduce the number of dimensions so that intuitions we have about low dimensional spaces would still hold true. The accuracy or performance of algorithms usually suffer when the number of dimensions increase. This is known as the curse of dimensionality.

Naive Bayes

Applications of Naive Bayes

Naive Bayes algorithm is an eager learning algorithm based on Bayes theorem with the assumption that all features are independent given the class label. Naive Bayes algorithm is well suited to text classification as its test time prediction is quick and as a result it can be deployed on a large dataset for inference.

Naive Bayes is usually used in applications where predictions are desired in real time such as fraud detection on credit card transactions. In these applications, a classifier that is capable of performing almost instantaneously is desired. Naive Bayes is also used extensively in text classification, spam filtering and sentiment analysis. In spam filtering, the words of an email or text message serve as the input features to the model, with each word assumed to be independent of others. Naive Bayes usually produces good results when this independent assumption holds true and coupled with its short inference time is sometimes preferred over more complicated classifiers.

Another area where Naive Bayes algorithm is widely used is in multi-class classification. In this domain, multiple classes or categories can be predicted given input features, with probabilities assigned to the predicted classes.

How to Build a Basic Model Using Naive Bayes in Python

For our hands on example we would build a Naive Bayes model in Python to tackle a spam classification problem. We would use the SMS spam collection dataset which is a set of 5,574 English text messages annotated to indicate the category. There are two categories - ham or legitimate messages and spam. The dataset can be downloaded from the following URL (https://www.kaggle.com/uciml/sms-spam-collection-dataset/downloads/spam.csv/1).

We would use the multinomial Naive Bayes classifier from Scikit-Learn machine learning library. As always, we begin by importing the libraries we would utilize.

```
import numpy as np
import pandas as pd
import matplotlib.pyplot as plt
# comment the magic command below if not running in Jupyter notebook
%matplotlib inline
```

Next we load the dataset using Pandas and display the first 5 rows.

```
data = pd.read_csv('spam.csv', encoding='latin-1')
data.head(5)
```

	v1		v2	Unnamed: 2	Unnamed: 3	Unnamed: 4
0	ham	Go until jurong point, crazy.. Available only ...	NaN	NaN	NaN	NaN
1	ham	Ok lar... Joking wif u oni...	NaN	NaN	NaN	NaN
2	spam	Free entry in 2 a wkly comp to win FA Cup fina...	NaN	NaN	NaN	NaN
3	ham	U dun say so early hor... U c already then say...	NaN	NaN	NaN	NaN
4	ham	Nah I don't think he goes to usf, he lives aro...	NaN	NaN	NaN	NaN

The column "v1" contains the class labels while "v2" are the contents of the SMS which we would use as the features of our model.

Let us plot a bar chart to visualize the distribution of legitimate and spam messages.

```
count_class = pd.value_counts(data['v1'], sort= True)
count_class.plot(kind='bar', color=[['blue', 'red']])
plt.title('Bar chart')
plt.show()
```

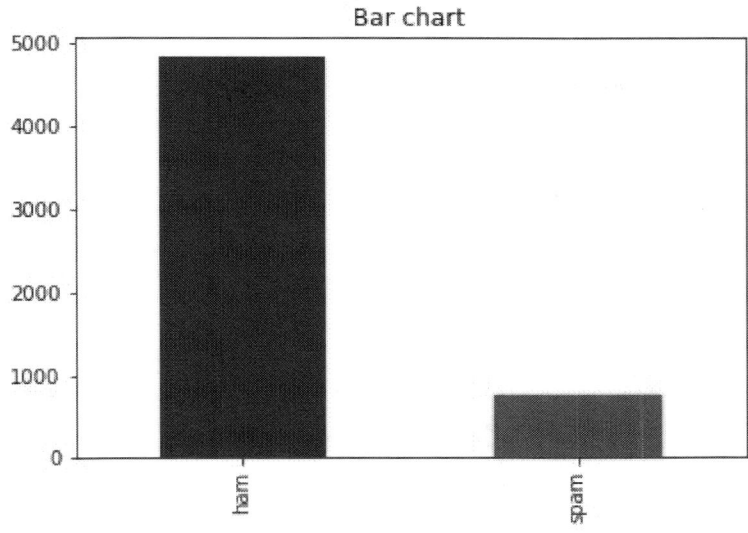

Bar chart

The words cannot be fed directly into the model as the features, so we have to vectorize them to create new features. We do this by considering the frequency of words after removing words that commonly appear in English sentences like "the", "a", "of" etc. We can do this feature extraction easily by using Scikit-Learn.

```
from sklearn.feature_extraction.text import CountVectorizer

f = CountVectorizer(stop_words = 'english')
X = f.fit_transform(data["v2"])
print(np.shape(X))
```

```
(5572, 8404)
```

After vectorization, 8,404 new features are created.

Next we map our target variables into categories and split the dataset into train and test sets.

```
from sklearn.model_selection import train_test_split

data["v1"]=data["v1"].map({'spam':1,'ham':0})
X_train, X_test, y_train, y_test = train_test_split(X,
data['v1'], test_size=0.25, random_state=42)
```

The next step involves initializing the Naive Bayes model and training it on the data.

```
from sklearn.naive_bayes import MultinomialNB

clf = MultinomialNB()
clf.fit(X_train, y_train)
```

Finally, we gauge the model performance on the test set.

```
score = clf.score(X_test, y_test)
```

```
print('Accuracy: {}'.format(score))
```

```
Accuracy: 0.976
```

The Naive Bayes classifier attains an accuracy of 0.976, which means that it predicted the correct class for 97.6% of samples.

Regression

Simple and Multiple Linear Regression

Regression involves finding the relationship between variables. Regression is typically used for predicting a single real value given a bunch of predictors. In simple regression, there are only two variables. The first is the independent variable while the other is the dependent variable. The regression task is thus to model how much the dependent variable changes with a change in the independent variable. A straight line equation may be used to fit a set of data points to capture the relationship between both variables. This is a case of a simple regression and the linear equation used is given below.

$$y = ax + b$$

The coefficient to be calculated is denoted by a while b is the intercept or bias of the model, x and y are the independent and dependent variables respectively.

In multiple linear regression, there are two or more independent variables, that is the number of predictors which determine the outcome y, are more than one. The relationship is still linear but y is dependent on more variables.

$$y = a_0 + a_1 x_1 + a_2 x_2 + a_3 x_3 + \cdots$$

Let us now look at a practical example. We would use the regression techniques explained above to predict the price of a house in a neighborhood given information about the house in the form of features. The dataset we would use is the Boston house pricing dataset and it contains 506 observations. The dataset can be downloaded from this URL (https://forge.scilab.org/index.php/p/rdataset/source/file/master/csv/MASS/Boston.csv).

First we import relevant libraries and load the dataset using Pandas.

```
import numpy as np
import pandas as pd
import matplotlib.pyplot as plt
# matplotlib magic command for Jupyter notebook
%matplotlib inline


dataset = pd.read_csv('Boston.csv')
dataset.head()
```

Unnamed: 0		crim	zn	indus	chas	nox	rm	age	dis	rad	tax	ptratio	black	lstat	medv
0	1	0.00632	18.0	2.31	0	0.538	6.575	65.2	4.0900	1	296	15.3	396.90	4.98	24.0
1	2	0.02731	0.0	7.07	0	0.469	6.421	78.9	4.9671	2	242	17.8	396.90	9.14	21.6
2	3	0.02729	0.0	7.07	0	0.469	7.185	61.1	4.9671	2	242	17.8	392.83	4.03	34.7
3	4	0.03237	0.0	2.18	0	0.458	6.998	45.8	6.0622	3	222	18.7	394.63	2.94	33.4
4	5	0.06905	0.0	2.18	0	0.458	7.147	54.2	6.0622	3	222	18.7	396.90	5.33	36.2

The dataset has 13 predictors such as the number of rooms in the house, age of house, pupil-teacher ratio in the town etc.

Let us plot the relationship between one of the predictors and the price of a house to see whether we can come up with any explanation from the visualization. The predictor we would use is the per capita crime rate by town which captures the rate of crime in the neighborhood.

```
plt.scatter(dataset['crim'], dataset['medv'])
plt.xlabel('Per capita crime rate by town')
plt.ylabel('Price')
plt.title("Prices vs Crime rate")
```

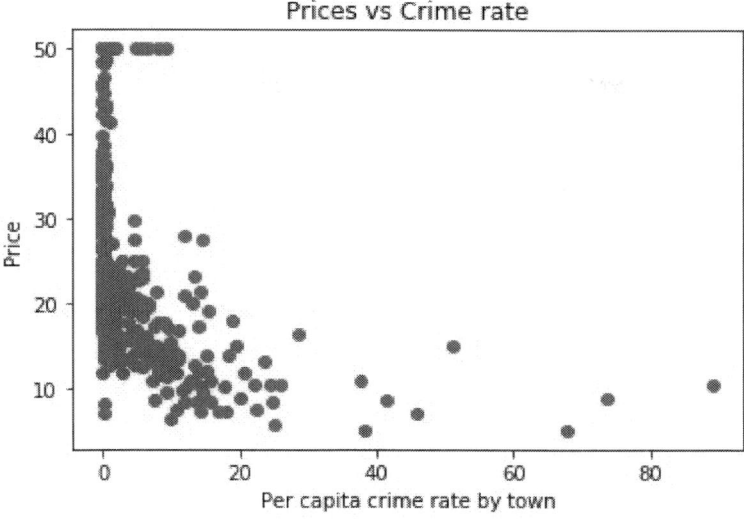

We can see that for towns with very low crime rates (at the beginning of the plot), there are houses for the full range of prices, both cheap and expensive. This is denoted by the vertical spread of points across the y axis. If we exclude the first 10 units on the x-axis, we notice that there is a negative correlation between price and the crime rate. This is hardly surprising as we would expect the price of houses to drop as the crime rate in the neighborhood increases.

Next we split our dataset into predictors and targets. Then we create a training and test set.

```
X = dataset.drop(['Unnamed: 0', 'medv'], axis=1)
y = dataset['medv']
```

```
from sklearn.model_selection import train_test_split
```

```
x_train, x_test, y_train, y_test = train_test_split(X, y,
test_size=0.3)
```

The next step involves importing the linear regression classifier from Scikit-Learn, initializing it and fitting the classifier on data.

```
# import linear regression classifier, initialize and fit the
model
```

```
from sklearn.linear_model import LinearRegression
```

```
regressor = LinearRegression()
regressor.fit(x_train, y_train)
```

Having fit the classifier, we can use it to predict house prices using features in the test set.

```
y_pred = regressor.predict(x_test)
```

The next step is to evaluate the classifier using metrics such as the mean square error and the coefficient of determination R square.

```
from sklearn.metrics import mean_squared_error, r2_score
```

```
# The coefficients
print('Coefficients: ¥n', regressor.coef_)
# The mean squared error
print('Mean                  squared                  error:
{:.2f}'.format(mean_squared_error(y_test, y_pred)))
# Explained variance score: 1 is perfect prediction
print('Variance score: {:.2f}'.format(r2_score(y_test, y_pred)))
```

```
Coefficients:
 [ -1.06335586e-01   4.02583336e-02   4.14059091e-02   3.26347638e+00
  -2.05940767e+01   4.07629939e+00  -1.16102163e-02  -1.65784773e+00
   2.80789477e-01  -1.07689848e-02  -9.48953794e-01   9.24511546e-03
  -5.13342800e-01]
Mean squared error: 22.01
Variance score: 0.72
```

The coefficients are the learnt parameters for each predictor,
the mean square error represents how far off our predictions
are from the actual values and variance score is the coefficient
of determination which gives the overall performance of the
model. A variance score of 1 is a perfect model, so it is clear
that with a score of 0.72, the model has learnt from the data.

Finally, we can plot the predicted prices from the model against
the ground truth (actual prices).

```
plt.scatter(y_test, y_pred)
```

```
plt.xlabel("Prices: $Y_i$")

plt.ylabel("Predicted prices: $\hat{Y}_i$")

plt.title("Prices vs Predicted prices: $Y_i$ vs $\hat{Y}_i$")
```

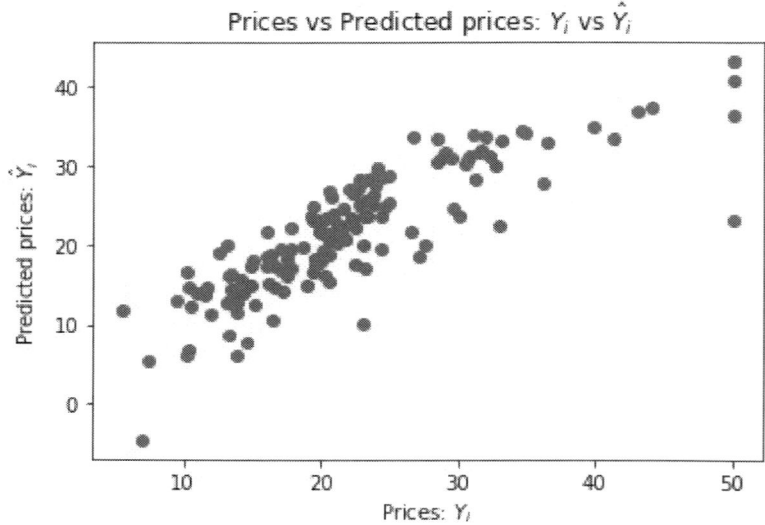

The scatter plot above shows a positive relationship between the predicted prices and actual prices. This indicates that our model has successfully captured the underlying relationship and can map from input features to output prices.

Here is the code in its entirety.

```
# import libraries
import numpy as np
```

```python
import pandas as pd
import matplotlib.pyplot as plt
%matplotlib inline

# load dataset
dataset = pd.read_csv('Boston.csv')
dataset.head()

# plot crime vs price
plt.scatter(dataset['crim'], dataset['medv'])
plt.xlabel('Per capita crime rate by town')
plt.ylabel('Price')
plt.title("Prices vs Crime rate")

# separate predictors and targets
X = dataset.drop(['Unnamed: 0', 'medv'], axis=1)
y = dataset['medv']

from sklearn.model_selection import train_test_split
x_train, x_test, y_train, y_test = train_test_split(X, y,
test_size=0.3)

# import linear regression classifier, initialize and fit the
model
from sklearn.linear_model import LinearRegression
```

```
regressor = LinearRegression()
regressor.fit(x_train, y_train)


y_pred = regressor.predict(x_test)


from sklearn.metrics import mean_squared_error, r2_score


# The coefficients
print('Coefficients: ¥n', regressor.coef_)
# The mean squared error
print('Mean                squared                error:
{:.2f}'.format(mean_squared_error(y_test, y_pred)))
# Explained variance score: 1 is perfect prediction
print('Variance score: {:.2f}'.format(r2_score(y_test, y_pred)))


# plot predicted prices vs actual prices
plt.scatter(y_test, y_pred)
plt.xlabel("Prices: $Y_i$")
plt.ylabel("Predicted prices: $¥hat{Y}_i$")
plt.title("Prices vs Predicted prices: $Y_i$ vs $¥hat{Y}_i$")
```

Logistic Regression

Logistic regression despite its name is a classification algorithm. Logistic regression is used when the dependent variable is binary in nature, that is when it can be either one of two values (categories) example true or false. It is a linear combination of weighted input features applied to the sigmoid function. The logit or sigmoid function is at the heart of logistic regression and models data along the range of 0 to 1.

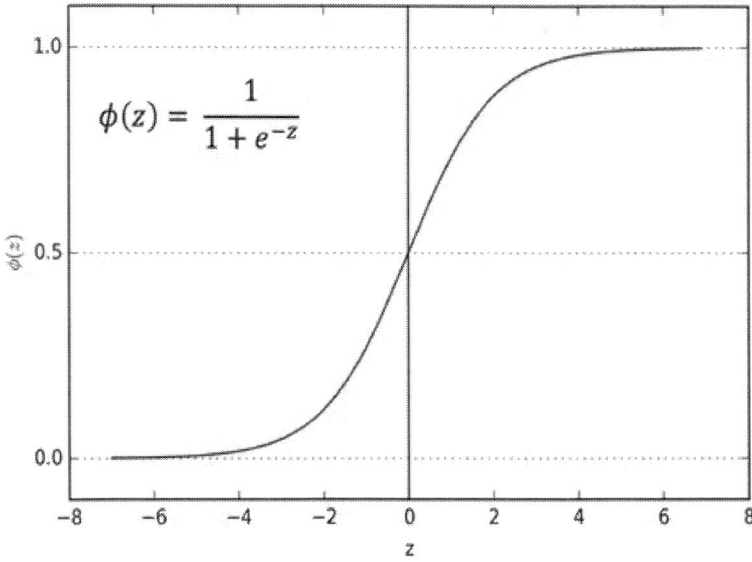

In the image above, z represents the weighted input features. What this means is that z is a linear addition of input features and the importance of input features (how large they are), is influenced by their weights (coefficients). A threshold is usually set to separate samples into classes. The threshold can be seen as the decision boundary. After the linear computation and the application of the sigmoid or logit function, the resultant value is compared to the threshold value. If it is equal to or larger than the threshold value, then the sample under consideration belongs to the positive class else it belongs to the negative class. The threshold value is usually set to 0.5.

Outputs from logistic regression can be interpreted as probabilities that show how likely a data point belongs to a category. The formula for the logistic function is shown below.

$$p(x) = \frac{1}{1 + e^{-(\beta_0 + \beta_1 x)}}$$

The main difference between logistic regression and simple regression is that logistic regression is used for classification when there can only be two classes (negative or positive) while simple regression is used to predict an actual value like a continuous number and not classes or categories.

We would now apply logistic regression to a binary classification problem. The dataset we would leverage is the Pima Indian Diabetes Database which is a dataset from the National Institute of Diabetes and Digestive and Kidney Diseases. The dataset contains a target variable that is used to indicate whether a patient developed diabetes or not. Our task is therefore to use diagnostic measurements as predictors to determine the diabetes status of a patient.

The dataset can be downloaded at: https://www.kaggle.com/uciml/pima-indians-diabetes-database/data

Let us import relevant libraries and load the dataset to have a sense of what it contains.

```
import numpy as np
import pandas as pd
import matplotlib.pyplot as plt

dataset = pd.read_csv('diabetes.csv')
dataset.head(5)
```

	Pregnancies	Glucose	BloodPressure	SkinThickness	Insulin	BMI	DiabetesPedigreeFunction	Age	Outcome
0	6	148	72	35	0	33.6	0.627	50	1
1	1	85	66	29	0	26.6	0.351	31	0
2	8	183	64	0	0	23.3	0.672	32	1
3	1	89	66	23	94	28.1	0.167	21	0
4	0	137	40	35	168	43.1	2.288	33	1

The dataset has 8 predictors such as glucose level of patient, age, skin thickness, body mass index, insulin level, age etc. These form the features for our model or in regression speak, the independent variables.

Next we separate the columns in the dataset into features and labels. The labels or class are represented by the "Outcome" column.

121

```
features = dataset.drop(['Outcome'], axis=1)
labels = dataset['Outcome']


from sklearn.model_selection import train_test_split
features_train,  features_test,  labels_train,  labels_test  =
train_test_split(features, labels, test_size=0.25)
```

The next step is to initialize a logistic regression model and fit
it to the Pima Indians diabetes data.

```
# Training the model
from sklearn.linear_model import LogisticRegression
classifier = LogisticRegression()


classifier.fit(features_train, labels_train)
```

The trained model can now be evaluated on the test set.

```
pred = classifier.predict(features_test)


from sklearn.metrics import accuracy_score
accuracy = accuracy_score(labels_test, pred)
print('Accuracy: {:.2f}'.format(accuracy))
```

```
Accuracy: 0.72
```

The trained logistic regression model attains an accuracy of 72% on the test set.

Generalized Linear Models

Generalized linear models are an extension of linear models where the dependent variable does not belong to a normal or Gaussian distribution. Generalized linear models are capable of modelling more complicated relationships between the independent and dependent variables. GLMs can often model various probability distributions as such poisson, binomial, multinomial distributions etc. Logistic regression is an example of a generalized linear model where the dependent variable is modelled using a binomial distribution. This enables it to create a mapping from inputs to outputs, where the outputs are binary in nature.

Poisson regression is a generalized linear model that is used for modelling count data. Count data are integer values that can only be positive. Poisson regression assumes that the independent variable y, belongs to a Poisson distribution, which is a type of exponential probability distribution. The main difference between Poisson regression and linear regression is that linear regression assumes the outputs are drawn from a normal distribution whereas Poisson distribution assumes y comes from a Poisson distribution. The outputs in Poisson regression are modelled as shown below.

$$y^t \sim Po(y^t; \mu^t)$$

Generalized linear models are made up of three components, the random components which are the probability distribution of the output, the systematic component which describes the explanatory variables (X) or predictors and the link function, which specifies the relationship between explanatory variables and the random component.

Since the hyperparameters (weights) of Poisson regression cannot take negative values, they are transformed using natural logarithm to ensure they are always positive. The mean of Poisson distribution is stated mathematically as:

$$\log \mu^t = w^T x^t, \quad \mu^t = exp(w^T x^t)$$

The objective function or loss function that is used to train the model in order to discover learnable parameters is shown below:

$$Loss = -\log p(y|X, w) = \sum_{t} \mu^t - y^t \log\mu^t$$

For our hands on example, we would use the statsmodels package that provides various functions and classes for statistical modelling, statistical data exploration etc. We would use a bundled dataset from statsmodels, the Scottish vote dataset that contains records from the 1997 vote to give the Scottish parliament the rights to collect taxes. The dataset contains 8 explanatory variables (predictors) and 32 observations, one for each district.

First we import the Statsmodels package as shown below.

```
import statsmodels.api as sm
```

Next we load the dataset and extract the explanatory variable (X).

```
data = sm.datasets.scotland.load()
# data.exog is the independent variable X
data.exog = sm.add_constant(data.exog)
```

Similar to Scikit-Learn, we import the appropriate model and instantiate an object from it. In this case we specify a generalized linear model and set the distribution family to Poisson.

```
# Instantiate a poisson family model with the default link
function.
poisson_model       =       sm.GLM(data.endog,       data.exog,
family=sm.families.Poisson())
```

We then fit the model on the data.

```
poisson_results = poisson_model.fit()
```

We can now print a summary of results to better understand the trained model.

```
print(poisson_results.summary())
```

```
                 Generalized Linear Model Regression Results
==============================================================================
Dep. Variable:                      y   No. Observations:                   32
Model:                            GLM   Df Residuals:                       24
Model Family:                 Poisson   Df Model:                            7
Link Function:                    log   Scale:                             1.0
Method:                          IRLS   Log-Likelihood:                -97.798
Date:                Fri, 06 Jul 2018   Deviance:                       5.1846
Time:                        18:50:39   Pearson chi2:                     5.14
No. Iterations:                     4
==============================================================================
                 coef    std err          z      P>|z|      [0.025      0.975]
------------------------------------------------------------------------------
const          5.7793      1.477      3.913      0.000       2.885       8.674
x1            -0.0025      0.002     -1.183      0.237      -0.007       0.002
x2            -0.1046      0.068     -1.545      0.122      -0.237       0.028
x3             0.0045      0.004      1.285      0.199      -0.002       0.011
x4            -0.0069      0.005     -1.255      0.210      -0.018       0.004
x5          8.237e-06   1.58e-05      0.521      0.602   -2.27e-05    3.92e-05
x6             0.0310      0.032      0.980      0.327      -0.031       0.093
x7             0.0001   9.52e-05      1.286      0.198   -6.41e-05       0.000
==============================================================================
```

The summary contains values like the coefficients or weights for independent variables, standard error and z scores.

Decision Trees and Random Forest

The Entropy of a Partition

Entropy can be defined as the measure of uncertainty in a sequence of random events. It is the rate of disorderliness in a sample space and is directly opposed to knowledge. When the entropy of a system is high, the knowledge that can be derived from the system is low and vice versa. An intuitive understanding of entropy is thinking of it as the amount of questions required to ask to arrive at some knowledge. For example, if I picked a random number and you were trying to guess what number it is. Asking a question like, "Is it an odd number", reduces the possibilities space by half. This means that the entropy or the degree of uncertainty in trying to determine which number I choose is reduced. In the same vein, the amount of information gain is large because the question moved you closer to the answer by dividing the sample space. Entropy usually ranges from 0 to 1. A system with an entropy of 0 is highly stable and the knowledge that can be derived from such a system is high. In general terms, low entropy in a system indicates high knowledge while high entropy indicates low knowledge or instability.

Entropy can be represented mathematically as:

$$E(S) = \sum_{i=1}^{c} - p_i \log_2 p_i$$

The formula above is the negative sum of log probabilities of an event happening. Remember that probability indicates the confidence we have in an event occurring, therefore entropy is how surprising it would be, for a sequence of events to occur together.

In machine learning as we would see later with decision trees, the entropy of two or more attributes of a classifier is defined by:

$$E(T,X) = \sum_{c \in X} P(c)E(c)$$

Decision trees are a machine learning algorithm that rely heavily on the entropy of an attribute and the information gain to determine how to classify samples in a classification problem. Let us look at decision trees in depth in the next section.

Creating a Decision Tree

A decision tree is a machine learning algorithm which is mainly used for classification that constructs a tree of possibilities where the branches in the tree represents decisions and the leaves represents label classification. The purpose of a decision tree is to create a structure where samples in each branch are homogenous or of the same type. It does this by splitting samples in the training data according to specific attributes that increase homogeneity in branches. These attributes form the decision node along which samples are separated. The process continues until all sample are correctly predicted as represented by the leaves of the tree.

To explain the concept of a decision tree further, let us look at a toy example below that demonstrates its capability.

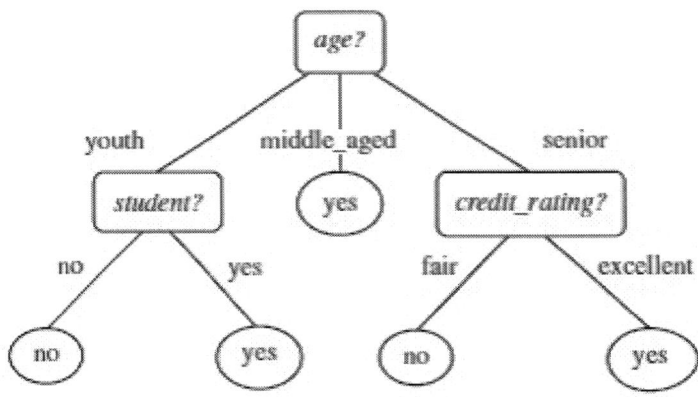

Let us assume that we are a laptop manufacturer and we want to predict which customers from an online store are likely to buy our new top of the range laptop, so that we can focus our marketing efforts accordingly. This problem can be modelled using a decision tree with two classes (yes or no), for whether a person is likely to purchase or not.

At the root of the tree, we want to choose an attribute about customers that reduces entropy the most. As we saw in the last section, by reducing the entropy, we increase the amount of knowledge that is contained in the system. We choose the appropriate attribute by calculating the entropy of each branch and the entropy of the targets (yes or no). The information gain is closely related to the entropy and is defined as the difference in entropy of the targets (final entropy) and the entropy given a particular attribute was chosen as the root node.

$$Gain(T, X) = Entropy(T) - Entropy(T, X)$$

The formula above is used to calculate the decrease in entropy. The attribute with the largest information gain or decrease in entropy is chosen as the root node. This means that the attribute reduces the decision space the most when compared to other attributes. The process is repeated to find other decision nodes via attributes until all samples are correctly classified through the leaves of the decision tree.

In the example above, age is the attribute that offers the most information gain so samples are split on that decision node. If the customer is middle aged, then they are likely to purchase a new laptop as they are probably working and have higher spending power. If the customer is a youth this brings us to another decision node. The attribute used is whether the youth is a student or not. If the youth is a student, they are likely to buy else they are not. That brings us to the leaves (classes) of the node following the youth branch of the tree. For the senior branch, we again split samples on an informative attribute, in this case credit rating. If the senior has an excellent credit rating that means they are likely to buy, else the leaf or classification for that sample along this branch of the tree is no.

Let us now work on an example using Python, Scikit-Learn and decision trees. We would tackle a multi-class classification problem where the the challenge is to classify wine into three types using features such as alcohol, color intensity, hue etc. The data we would use comes from the wine recognition dataset by UC Irvine. It can be downloaded at https://gist.github.com/tijptjik/9408623/archive/b237fa584 8349a14a14e5d4107dc7897c21951f5.zip

First, lets load the dataset and use Pandas **head** method to have a look at it.

```
import numpy as np

import pandas as pd

import matplotlib.pyplot as plt

# comment the magic command below if not running in Jupyter
notebook

%matplotlib inline


dataset = pd.read_csv('wine.csv')

dataset.head(5)
```

Wine	Alcohol	Malic.acid	Ash	Acl	Mg	Phenols	Flavanoids	Nonflavanoid.phenols	Proanth	Color.int	Hue	OD	Proline
0	1	14.23	1.71	2.43	15.6	127	2.80	3.06	0.28	2.29	5.64	1.04	3.92	1065
1	1	13.20	1.78	2.14	11.2	100	2.65	2.76	0.26	1.28	4.38	1.05	3.40	1050
2	1	13.16	2.36	2.67	18.6	101	2.80	3.24	0.30	2.81	5.68	1.03	3.17	1185
3	1	14.37	1.95	2.50	16.8	113	3.85	3.49	0.24	2.18	7.80	0.86	3.45	1480
4	1	13.24	2.59	2.87	21.0	118	2.80	2.69	0.39	1.82	4.32	1.04	2.93	735

There are 13 predictors and the first column "wine" contains the targets. The next thing we do is split the dataset into predictors and targets, sometimes referred to as features and labels respectively.

```
features = dataset.drop(['Wine'], axis=1)
labels = dataset['Wine']
```

As is the custom to ensure good evaluation of our model, we divide the dataset into a train and test split.

```
from sklearn.model_selection import train_test_split
features_train, features_test, labels_train, labels_test = train_test_split(features, labels, test_size=0.25)
```

All that is left is for us to import the decision tree classifier and fit it to our data.

```
from sklearn.tree import DecisionTreeClassifier
classifier = DecisionTreeClassifier()

classifier.fit(features_train, labels_train)
```

We can now evaluate the trained model on the test set and print out the accuracy.

```
pred = classifier.predict(features_test)

from sklearn.metrics import accuracy_score
accuracy = accuracy_score(labels_test, pred)
print('Accuracy: {:.2f}'.format(accuracy))
```

```
Accuracy: 0.91
```

We achieve an accuracy of 0.91 which is very impressive. It means that 91% of samples in our test set were correctly classified.

Random Forests

Random forests are a type of ensemble model. An ensemble model is one which is constructed from other models. This means that it is a combination of several weak learners to form a strong learner. The prediction of an ensemble model may be the average or weighted average of all learners that it is comprised of.

Random forests are an extension of decision trees whereby several decision trees are grown to form a forest. The final prediction of a random forest model is a combination of all component decision trees. For regression it may be a simple average of outputs or a label vote in the case of classification. Though random forest are made of several decision trees, each decision tree is trained on a subset of data that is randomly selected hence the name random forest. The other trick of random forest is that unlike a decision tree where the best attribute is chosen in order to split samples at a decision node from all available attributes, random forest only picks the best attribute from a subset of randomly chosen attributes for each decision node. As a result, each node in a tree is not deterministic, that is for each time we run the algorithm, we are likely to end up with different tree structures. However, the most informative attributes still find their way to trees in the forest and are present across many trees. This makes the results of the random forest algorithm to be less prone to errors due to variations in the input data.

The subset of data on which a decision tree that makes up a random forest is trained on is called bagged data and is usually around 60% of the entire dataset. The remainder on which the performance of individuals trees are tested on is known as the out-of-bag data. Therefore each tree in the forest is trained and evaluated on a different subset of data through the randomization process.

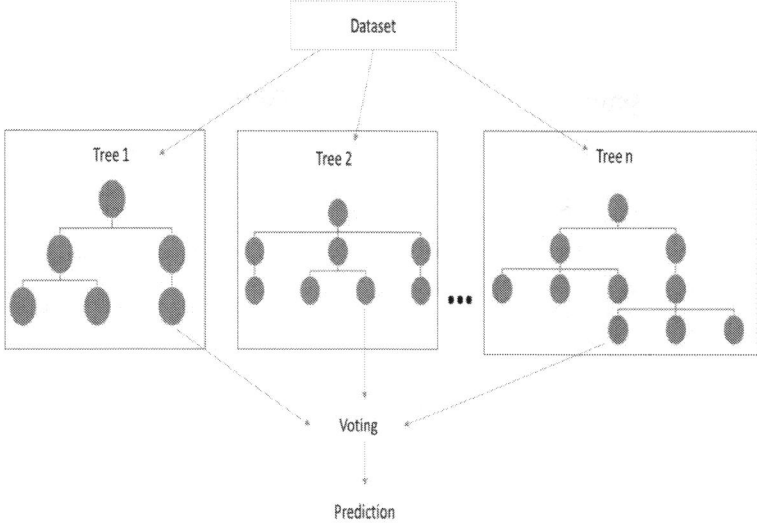

The image above shows a pictorial representation of random forests. It is made up of several trees trained on different instances of the dataset. The attributes in each decision node are also randomized. Finally, the output prediction is an ensemble of the classification of each decision tree.

We would now try out a random forest classifier on the wine dataset and compare its performance on the test set to the decision tree model in the previous section. The beautiful thing about using machine learning models from Scikit-Learn is that the APIs to train and test a model are the same regardless of the algorithm being used. So you would notice that we only need to import the correct classifier, initialize it and all other portions of code would remain unchanged. We are already familiar with how parts of the code works so here is the code for random forest in full.

135

```python
import numpy as np
import pandas as pd

# load dataset
dataset = pd.read_csv('wine.csv')

# separate features and labels
features = dataset.drop(['Wine'], axis=1)
labels = dataset['Wine']

# split dataset into train and test sets
from sklearn.model_selection import train_test_split
features_train, features_test, labels_train, labels_test = train_test_split(features, labels, test_size=0.25)

# import random forest classifier from sklearn
from sklearn.ensemble import RandomForestClassifier
classifier = RandomForestClassifier()

# fit classifier on data
classifier.fit(features_train, labels_train)

# predict classes of test set samples
pred = classifier.predict(features_test)
```

```
# evaluate classifier performance using accuracy metric
from sklearn.metrics import accuracy_score
accuracy = accuracy_score(labels_test, pred)
print('Accuracy: {:.2f}'.format(accuracy))
```

```
Accuracy: 0.98
```

We achieve an accuracy of 98% on the test set which is a massive jump from 91% when we used a decision tree classifier. We can see that the randomization approach of random forest enables the algorithm to generalize better hence higher accuracy is recorded on the test set.

Neural Networks

Perceptrons

The perceptron is a binary linear classifier that is only capable of predicting classes of samples if those samples can be separated via a straight line. The perceptron algorithm was introduced by Frank Rosenblatt in 1957. It classifies samples using hand crafted features which represents information about the samples, weighs the features on how important they are to the final prediction and the resulting computation is compared against a threshold value.

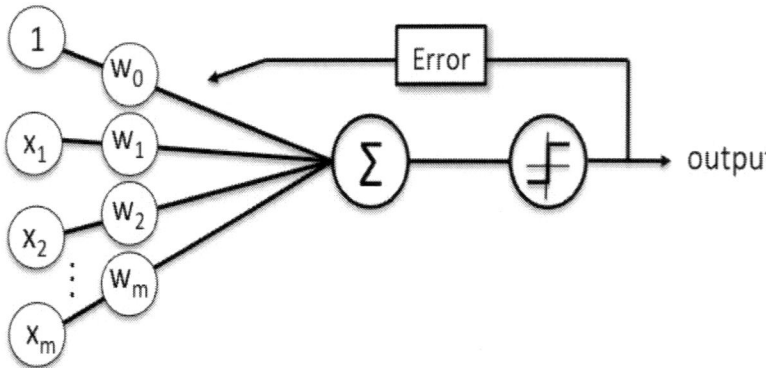

In the image above, X represents the inputs to the model and W represents the weights (how important are individual features). A linear computation of the weighted sum of features is carried out during the formula below:

$$z = w_0 x_0 + w_1 x_1 + \ldots + w_m x_m$$

The value of z is then passed through a step function to predict the class of the sample. A step function is an instant transformation of a value from 0 to 1. What this means is that if z is greater than or equal to 0, its predicts one class, else it predicts the other. The step function can be represented mathematically as:

$$f(x) = \begin{cases} 1 & \text{if } \mathbf{w} \cdot \mathbf{x} + b > 0 \\ 0 & \text{otherwise} \end{cases}$$

At each iteration, the predicted class gets compared to the actual class and the weights gets updated if the prediction was wrong else it is left unchanged in the case of a correct prediction. Updates of weights continue until all samples are correctly predicted, at which point we can say that the perceptron classifier has found a linear decision boundary that perfectly separates all samples into two mutually exclusive classes.

During training the weights are updated by adding a small value to the original weights. The amount added is determined by the perceptron learning rule. The weight update process can be experienced mathematically as shown below.

$$w_j := w_j + \Delta w_j$$

The amount by which weights are updated is given by the perceptron learning rule below.

$$\Delta w_j = \eta \left(y^{(i)} - \hat{y}^{(i)} \right) x_j^{(i)}$$

The first coefficient on the right hand side of the equation is called the learning rate and acts as a scaling factor to increase or decrease the extent of the update. The intuitive understanding of the above equation is that with each pass through the training set, the weights of misclassified examples are nudged in the correct direction so that the value of z can be such that the step function correctly classifies the sample. It should be noted that the perceptron learning algorithm described is severely limited as it can only learn simple functions that have a clear linear boundary. The perceptron is almost never used in practice but served as an integral building block during the earlier development of artificial neural networks.

Modern iterations are known as multi-layer perceptrons. Multi-layer perceptrons are feed forward neural networks that have several nodes in the structure of a perceptron. However, there are important differences. A multilayer perceptron is made up of multiple layers of neurons stacked to form a network. The activation functions used are non-linear unlike the perceptron model that uses a step function. Nonlinear activations are capable of capturing more interesting representations of data and as such do not require input data to be linearly separable. The other important difference is that multi-layer perceptrons are trained using a different kind of algorithm called backpropagation which enables training across multiple layers.

Backpropagation

Backpropagation is an algorithm technique that is used to solve the issue of credit assignment in artificial neural networks. What that means is that it is used to determine how much an input's features and weights contribute to the final output of the model. Unlike the perceptron learning rule, backpropagation is used to calculate the gradients, which tell us how much a change in the parameters of the model affects the final output. The gradients are used to train the model by using them as an error signal to indicate to the model how far off its predictions are from the ground truth. The backpropagation algorithm can be thought of as the chain rule of derivatives applied across layers.

Let us look at a full fledged illustration of a multi-layer perceptron to understand things further.

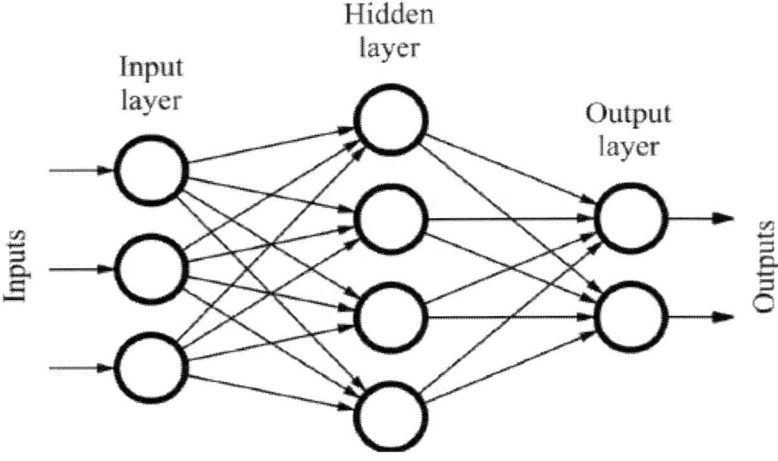

The network above is made up of three layers, the input layer which are the features fed into the network, the hidden layer which is so called because we cannot observe what goes on inside and the output layer, through which we get the prediction of the model. During training, in order to calculate by how each node contributes to the final prediction and adjust them accordingly to yield a higher accuracy across samples, we need to change the weights using the backpropagation algorithm. It is the weights that are learned during the training process hence they are sometimes referred to as the learnable parameters of the model. To visually understand what goes on during backpropagation, lets us look at the image of a single node below.

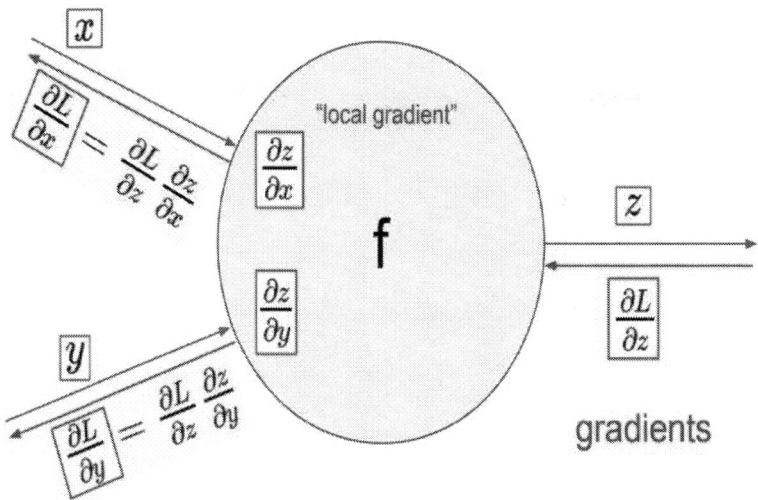

In the node above x and y are the input features while f is the nonlinear activation function. During training computations are calculated in a forward fashion from the inputs, across the hidden layers, all the way to the output. This is known as the forward pass denoted by green arrows in the image. The prediction of the model is then compared to the ground truth and the error is propagated backwards. This is known as the backward pass and assigns the amount by which every node is responsible for the computed error through the backpropagation algorithm. It is depicted with red arrows in the image above. This process continues until the model finds a set of weights that captures the underlying data representation and correctly predicts majority of samples.

Clustering

Implementation of the Model

Clustering is a type of unsupervised learning technique in which there are no explicit labels. Clustering is used to discover groups of data points in a dataset. A group or cluster is made up of members that are similar to each other but are collectively different from other clusters. A good clustering algorithm must have the ability to discover some or all hidden clusters in a dataset, should exhibit in cluster similarity but different clusters should be dissimilar or far from each other. The clustering algorithm should also be scalable to larger datasets and should be able to handle noisy data points and outliers.

There are two main categories of clustering algorithms - hierarchical clustering algorithms and partitive clustering algorithms. In hierarchical clustering, there is a clear relationship between discovered clusters. This can take the form of a hierarchy or order. Whereas in partitive algorithms, the relationship between clusters is not clear and it is sometimes referred to as having a flat structure. Clustering algorithms can also be seen from another perspective. Algorithms that allow a data point to belong to more than one cluster are known as soft clustering algorithms. In such a process, probabilities are assigned to each data point to indicate how likely it belongs to any particular cluster. Hard clustering algorithms on the other hand, require that data points only belong to exactly one cluster.

Hierarchical clustering algorithms are deterministic, which means that each time the algorithm is deployed on a dataset, we are bound to find the same clusters. This enables reproducibility of results. Partitive algorithms are non-deterministic and would produce a slightly different cluster representation with every run through the dataset.

Bottom-up Hierarchical Clustering

Bottom-up hierarchical clustering is a type of hierarchical clustering technique whereby every data point begins in a cluster of its own. A distance measure such as Euclidean distance is then used to calculate the distance of all points from one another. The points with the shortest distance are merged to form a cluster of their own. The process continues until all points belong to one big cluster. The intuition is that data points which are similar are likely to be separated by a small distance in the feature space.

A popular type of bottom-up clustering is the hierarchical agglomerative clustering algorithm. Here the distance measure may be Euclidean, Manhattan or Minkowski distance. When clusters are created, the distance between clusters may be the shortest distance between any two points in both clusters, known as single linkage, the farthest distance between two points, referred to as complete linkage or it may be an average of the distance of all data points in both clusters (average linkage).

Below is the mathematical expression for single linkage as described above.

$$L(r,s) = \min(D(x_{ri}, x_{sj}))$$

Where D is the distance measure example Manhattan distance. Manhattan distance can be expressed mathematically as:

$$\sum_{i=1}^{k} |x_i - y_i|$$

Let us look at an image of a dendrogram, which is just the way clusters are represented when using an hierarchical agglomerative clustering algorithm.

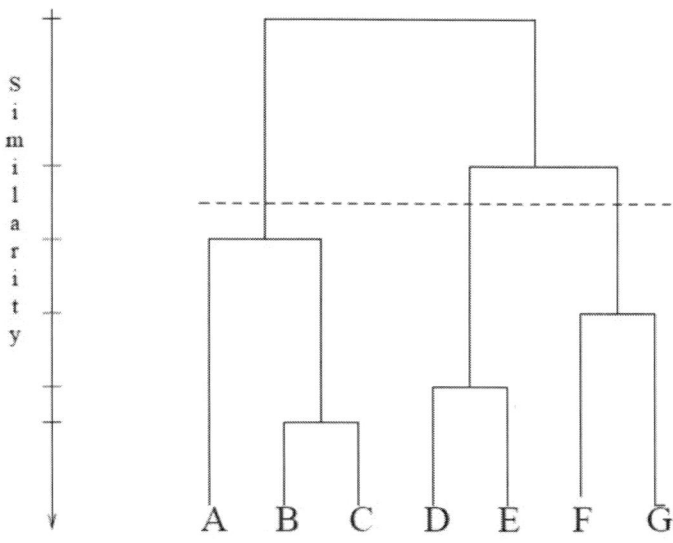

In the dendrogram, each point (A through G) starts in a cluster of their own. Then they are merged into clusters with other points which they are not far away from. The process proceeds in a bottom-up fashion and the height represents the similarity between clusters at the point they were merged. After all data points are grouped as one cluster, a threshold value may be passed to trace back any number of clusters that is desired. This is represented as the horizontal line. There are therefore three clusters in the dendrogram above.

K-means Clustering

K-means is a partitive clustering algorithm that assigns data points into a predetermined number of clusters. The number of clusters must be passed as a metric to the algorithm. K-means works by randomly choosing centroids in a data distribution and assigning data points to centroids that they are closest to. The number of centroids is the same as the number of clusters to be determined. The centroids are then recomputed by taking the mean of all data points assigned to that centroid's cluster. The process is iterative. Data points are reassigned to centroids they are now closest to and the centroids are updated for each cluster. Convergence is achieved when data points are no longer reassigned to new clusters.

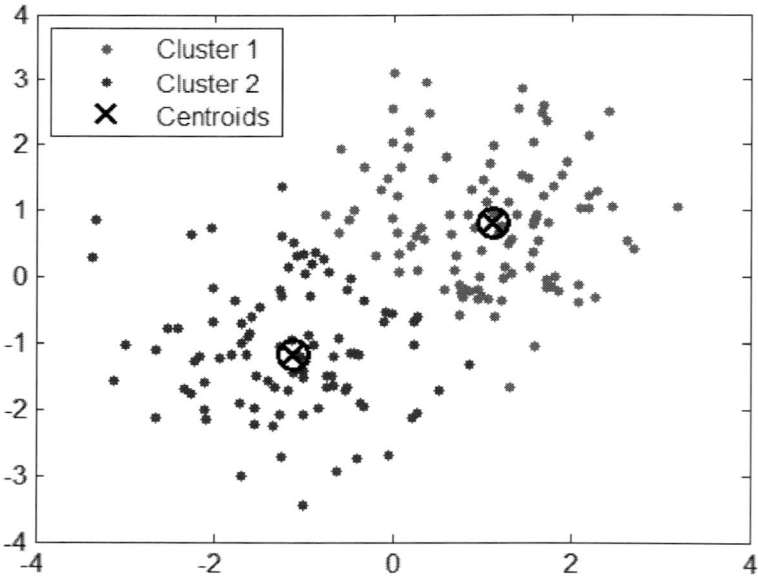

The above image shows an example of a converged dataset. There are two clusters and data points belongs to the cluster they are closest to. The center of each cluster is represented by its centroid. K-means algorithm is sensitive to the number of clusters and the initialization of centroids. Depending on how centroids are initialized, we would end up with different data points in various clusters. Since K-means requires that the number of clusters be passed as a metric, it is desirable to know what the optimum number of clusters would be for a dataset. This can be done using the elbow technique. Generally speaking, the error rate goes down rapidly as we increase the number of clusters until it saturates at a certain point where an increase in cluster size does not bring about a proportionate reduction in error. The elbow method tells us to choose as the optimum number of clusters the number of clusters for which the error rate has not plateaued.

Network Analysis

Betweenness centrality

Graphs are a type of data structure used to represent data that features high connectivity, that is the data has relationships that makes it connected. Network theory is the study of graphs as a way to understand the relationships between entities that made up a graph. Many kinds of analytical problems can be modelled as a graph problem, however it is best to use graphs when the data increases in complexity because of its interconnectedness. A very popular example of this kind of data is social media data which can be argued to possess an inherent network structure. Analysis of such data would not be well suited to traditional techniques as found in relational databases. Social media data can therefore be modelled as a graph network where vertices or nodes are connected to each other. Nodes could represent entities like people and edges could represent relationships. Modelling the data this way enables us to answer important questions about the nature of relationships between people and how people are likely to react to events given the reaction of their inner circle.

This brings us to the notion of centrality in network analysis. Centrality can be defined as determining which nodes or in our case people, are important to a particular network. Another way of framing this is, what node or entity is central to the way a network operates. There are many ways in which importance can be calculated in a network and these are known as centrality measures. Some of them are degree centrality, closeness centrality, betweenness centrality and eigenvector centrality.

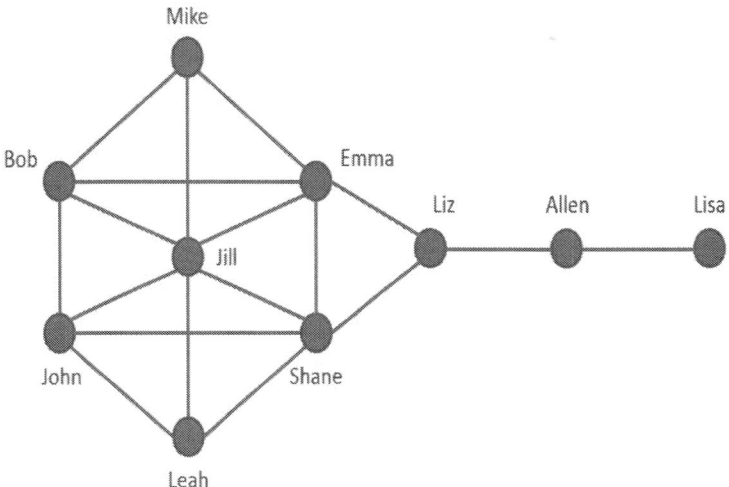

The image above is a network showing a graph representation of friends in a social context. The nodes represents individuals while the edges represents relationships. This is an example of an undirected graph. What that means is that the connections (edges) has no sense of direction. If we want to find out who is important in this network, we would use any of the centrality measures listed above.

Degree centrality is the number of edges connected to a node, it can be thought of as popularity or the exposure to the network. Even Though it is a very simple metric, it can be effective in some cases. Closeness centrality measures the average distance between a node and all other nodes in a network. It can be seen as having indirect influence on a network or the point through which information can be disseminated easily through a network.

Betweenness centrality measures how often a node is between the shortest path to any two randomly chosen nodes. In other words, betweenness is a measure of how many times a node acts as a bridge between the shortest path of any two nodes in the network. Betweenness centrality can be seen as conferring informal power on a node in terms of a node being a sort of gatekeeper or broker between parts of the network. Betweenness centrality of a node v can be expressed mathematically as:

$$Betwenness(v) = \sum_{s \neq v \neq t \in V} \frac{\sigma_{st}(v)}{\sigma_{st}}$$

Where the denominator is the total number of the shortest paths from nodes s to t and the numerator is the number of those shortest paths that go through node v.

Eigenvector Centrality

Eigenvector centrality is a centrality measure that not only considers how many nodes a particular node is connected to, but factors in the quality or importance of such nodes in its calculation. Intuitively, eigenvector centrality measures "not what you know but who you know". So the centrality of every node is calculated based on the quality of its connections and not just the number of connections as is the case in degree centrality. Eigenvector centrality can be seen as a measure of the extent to which a node is connected to other influential nodes.

Google at its core uses the Pagerank algorithm which is a variant of eigenvector centrality to rank the relevancy of results based on users search queries. The intuition is that websites are modelled as nodes on a network and the entire world wide web is represented as one big network. Nodes (websites) would be ranked higher based on the quality or reputation of other websites that point to them. Merely increasing the number of links that point to a site does not increase its influence in terms of how it is ranked in search results. Links that point to a website have to come from important websites for the ranking of a particular website to increase. This is sensible as popular websites are more likely to point to the most relevant content. Eigenvector centrality is a powerful metric that is used in analyzing networks.

Recommender Systems

The information overload as occasioned by the internet has lead to a paralysis of sorts as users are overwhelmed with variety of choices. Recommender systems are a way through which information is filtered so that the most relevant content are shown to users. Recommender systems seek to predict the

153

preference a user would give to an item or product in light of their past interaction or behaviors on a platform. It is one of the most commercially viable use cases of machine learning as companies from Amazon to Netflix all have a business model that benefits enormously from showing relevant content to users in order to increase sales or interaction with their platforms.

Recommender systems are divided into three broad categories based on the techniques they employ. There are content based filtering, collaborative filtering and hybrid recommender systems. Content based filtering relies on the features of an item and a user's profile. Items are recommended based on how similar they are to a user's tastes. A movie for example may have features such as actors, genre, director etc. A user with particular preferences would get recommendations of movies whose features match the user's information.

Collaborative filtering makes use of a user's past behavior, preferences etc in combination with the preferences of other users to determine items that are recommended. Users are likely to appreciate items that are liked by other users with similar preferences.

Hybrid recommender systems combines approaches from content based filtering and collaborative filtering. They may be used to manage the shortcomings of any particular approach example when a new item is added and we do not yet have enough information about that item or when users have not had many interactions on the platform to be able to accurately gauge their preferences.

Thank you !

Thank you for buying this book! It is intended to help you understanding data science using Python. If you enjoyed this book and felt that it added value to your life, we ask that you please take the time to review it.

Your honest feedback would be greatly appreciated. It really does make a difference.

AI SCIENCES

We are a very small publishing company and our survival depends on your reviews.
Please, take a minute to write us an honest review.

Sources & References

We're almost done here. But if you want to dig deeper and satisfy your curiosity about Python, data science, machine learning, deep learning, and artificial intelligence, here again are some of the useful resources for you:

Software, libraries, & programming language

- Python (https://www.python.org/)
- Anaconda (https://anaconda.org/)
- Virtualenv (https://virtualenv.pypa.io/en/stable/)
- Jupyter (http://jupyter.org/)
- Numpy (http://www.numpy.org/)
- Pandas (https://pandas.pydata.org/)
- Matplotlib (https://matplotlib.org/)
- Scikit-learn (http://scikit-learn.org/)
- Statsmodels (https://www.statsmodels.org/stable/index.html)
- TensorFlow (https://www.tensorflow.org/)
- TFLearn (http://tflearn.org/)

Datasets

- Kaggle (https://www.kaggle.com/datasets)
- Boston Housing Dataset (https://forge.scilab.org/index.php/p/rdataset/source/file/master/csv/MASS/Boston.csv)
- Pima Indians Diabetes Database (https://www.kaggle.com/uciml/pima-indians-diabetes-database/data)

- Iris Dataset
  (https://www.kaggle.com/saurabh00007/iriscsv/downloads/Iris.csv/1)
- Spam Dataset
  (http://www.dt.fee.unicamp.br/~tiago/smsspamcollection)
- Scottish Vote
  (http://www.statsmodels.org/dev/datasets/generated/scotland.html)

Online books, tutorials, & other references

- Udacity Intro to Machine Learning
  (https://www.udacity.com/course/intro-to-machine-learning--ud120)
- Coursera Machine Learning
  (https://www.coursera.org/learn/machine-learning)
- Coursera Deep Learning Specialization
  (https://www.coursera.org/specializations/deep-learning)
- fast.ai - Deep Learning for Coders
  (http://course.fast.ai/)
- Machine Learning Mastery
  (https://machinelearningmastery.com/a-gentle-introduction-to-scikit-learn-a-python-machine-learning-library/)
- Bayes' Theorem (https://brilliant.org/wiki/bayes-theorem/)
- Kaggle KNN Visualization Notebook
  (https://www.kaggle.com/skalskip/iris-data-visualization-and-knn-classification)

- Overfitting
  (https://en.wikipedia.org/wiki/Overfitting)
- A Neural Network Program
  (https://playground.tensorflow.org/)
- Analytics Vidhya Blog
  (https://www.analyticsvidhya.com/blog/)
- Machine Learning Crash Course by Google
  (https://playground.tensorflow.org/)
- Choosing the Right Estimator (http://scikit-learn.org/stable/tutorial/machine_learning_map/index.html)

Thank you !

Thank you for buying this book! It is intended to help you understanding data science using Python. If you enjoyed this book and felt that it added value to your life, we ask that you please take the time to review it.

Your honest feedback would be greatly appreciated. It really does make a difference.

AI SCIENCES

We are a very small publishing company and our survival depends on your reviews.
Please, take a minute to write us an honest review.

If you want to help us produce more material like this, then please leave an honest review on amazon. It really does make a difference.

https://www.amazon.com/dp/B07F7QC635

AI SCIENCES

Made in the USA
Middletown, DE
01 March 2019